ETHICAL BUSINESS

Cultivating the Good in Organizational Culture

RICHARD KYTE

ANSELM
ACADEMIC

For Lindy

Created by the publishing team of Anselm Academic.

Cover image: © Rawpixel.com / shutterstock.com

Printed in the United States of America

7075

ISBN 978-1-59982-630-1

"Richard Kyte's *Ethical Business* elevates business ethics from a process of rules-based problem solving to the practice of character-based relationship building. The author argues that ethical business leaders derive their power from trust, not coercion. The ethical businesses that Kyte describes reap the rewards of attracting more productive employees, more loyal customers, and more committed investors. Kyte provides a blueprint for building companies and brands in sync with today's increasingly socially conscious consumers."

—Frank J. Oswald
Lecturer, School of Professional Studies
Columbia University, New York

"Richard Kyte's *Ethical Business: Cultivating the Good in Organizational Culture* is an invaluable book that takes seriously the societal setting of business practices by using virtue approaches to engage business ethics. Kyte uses illuminating examples from real-world business leaders and companies, as well as from the news, literature, and films. His wise treatment of the roles of power, trust, and meaning will be especially useful for those who seek to reflect more deeply on how to create healthier working environments. I highly recommend this outstanding book for use in classrooms, board rooms, offices, and homes."

—Paul F. Jeffries, PhD
Associate Professor of Philosophy
Ripon College

"In *Ethical Business*, Richard Kyte has provided readers with an approach that departs significantly from most business ethics textbooks. Using vivid real-life examples, Kyte highlights the many critical aspects of an organization that contribute to an ethical culture. The book is well written and is useful for both the student of business ethics and the practicing manager."

—K. Praveen Parboteeah
University of Wisconsin—Whitewater

Author Acknowledgments

The danger of acknowledging one's gratitude is the very real risk of leaving out someone who should be included, and that is especially true in the case of a project like this, which is the result of countless conversations over the years about how healthy organizations are nurtured and maintained. Nevertheless, I would like to single out a few individuals—colleagues, friends, mentors, and students—who have been particularly helpful in bringing this collection of words and ideas to its present shape: Rick Artman, Matthew Bersagel-Braley, Maureen Cooney, Chuck Driscoll, Don Frick, Louise Hemstead, Tom Knothe, Rodney Nordeng, Amy Pehrson, Lindy Saline, Chris Scheuermann, Mark Shack, Dave Skogen, Tom Thibodeau, and Nicole Van Ert.

I would also like to thank Beth Erickson, Maura Hagarty, and Jerry Ruff of Anselm Academic, who shepherded this manuscript with patience, skill, and encouragement from beginning to end.

Publisher Acknowledgments

Thank you to the following individuals who reviewed this work in progress:

Patricia M. Calton, *Saint Mary's University of Minnesota*

Kyle Hubbard, *Saint Anselm College*

Patrick G. Somers, *Loyola University of Chicago*

Contents

Introduction 7

1. Growing Ethical Cultures 13
   The Classical Virtues   15
   The Limits of Compliance   21
   Communities of Character   30
   Conclusion   38

2. Ethical Leadership 41
   The Hawthorne Studies   42
   Human Nature   45
   Servant Leadership   51
   The Importance of Purpose   59
   Conclusion   68

3. Power, Trust, and Meaning 71
   Power   75
   Trust   83
   Meaning   92
   Conclusion   102

4. Ethical Decision Making 105
   How Ethical Reasoning Works   108
   The Four-Way Method   119
   Decision Making in Practice   128
   Conclusion   131

5. Exercising the Moral Imagination 134
   Case Study 1: The Would-Be Whistle-blower   135
   Case Study 2: Netflix and Ethics of Apology   144
   Case Study 3: A Conflict of Interest?   152
   Conclusion   158

Conclusion 161

Index 165

Introduction

What does it mean for an organization to be ethical? Does it mean simply that it does not get involved in scandals or that it doesn't break any laws? Or does it mean something more? For example, might it mean that the organization contributes something positive to society—by providing living wages for its employees, a reliable return on investment for its shareholders, or support for charitable organizations in communities? Might it mean even more? Might it mean that it provides meaning and purpose to the lives of its employees or that it enhances the life of the community in which the organization resides?

These are some of the questions raised in this book, and the answers provided draw upon an expansive view of ethics, considered not just as "doing the right thing" but also as living well or flourishing. If the goal is living well, then organizational ethics should focus not just on how to respond to problems as they occur but on how to create the working conditions under which people can flourish.

Work, after all, is central to most people's lives. American full-time employees work an average of forty-seven hours per week—spending more time working than on any other activity.[1] Without good working conditions—including a sense of worthwhile purpose, fair treatment by one's employer, respect and civility from one's colleagues, clients, or customers—it is difficult for the rest of one's life to go well. Good work is integral to a good life. And that is why ethics is not just about individuals doing "right things." It is also about organizations creating conditions in which life can be "good."

Some people are fortunate in their employment. Their work is energizing, fulfilling, and challenging. They look forward to going to work in the morning, and they come home at the end of the day full of satisfaction, eager to tell others about what they accomplished. They see their work as important, others regularly show appreciation

---

1. "The '40-Hour' Workweek Is Actually Longer—by Seven Hours," *Gallup*, August 29, 2014, *http://www.gallup.com/poll/175286/hour-workweek-actually-longer-seven-hours.aspx*.

for the contribution they make, and they have friends at work with whom they enjoy spending time.

And yet, far too many people struggle day after day, in frustration and stress, because they are treated unfairly, find little or no purpose in their work, or have to endure intimidation and uncertainty. They live lives of fear and discouragement, a condition Thoreau called "quiet desperation," and do not know what to do about it. They are afraid to say anything because they have no reason to think that things would improve and every reason to suppose that things will get worse if they speak up.

For most people, perhaps, work falls somewhere between these extremes, and at different stages in one's career, one is likely to experience periods of both fulfillment and discouragement.

What has all this got to do with ethics?

Everything. If one starts with the view that ethics is about the conditions of a good life, this is obvious. It is a view with a long history, beginning with Aristotle, who claimed that the highest good is happiness (or "flourishing") and that ethics is the study of the conditions that contribute to happiness.[2] It is not so obvious if one takes a more contemporary view of ethics, particularly applied ethics, which restricts ethics to resolution of conflicts stemming from serious disagreements.

Imagine Lisa, a recent graduate with a four-year degree in management from a reputable university. She lands a job in the human resources department of a company that operates several nursing homes. She enjoys the work and the people. The director of her office is demanding but fair, and she feels proud of herself as she begins to learn the ropes. The only thing troubling her is a disquieting feeling that everything may not be on the up and up. When visiting one of their sites, she overhears a conversation in which family members are told that Medicare eligibility could be extended by creating a "medical emergency" and hospitalizing the patient. Upon returning from the hospital, the patient's nursing home costs would be covered for an additional hundred days. This sounds to Lisa like fraud, but she isn't sure; the way the situation was discussed made the process seem

---

2. This view is known as "virtue ethics," and more will be said about it in subsequent chapters.

normal, as if it was something the nursing home administration did routinely. When she brings the matter up with her supervisor the next day, she is told bluntly, "That's not your concern. You just focus on what you were hired to do."

Situations like Lisa's are often referred to as "ethical dilemmas." She finds herself faced with a difficult question of the right thing to do, and yet, it is not the sort of dilemma that she recalls from her business ethics course the previous year. First of all, it is not even clear to her that anybody is acting unethically. She just overheard a bit of conversation, and she doesn't know much about Medicare requirements or even what sorts of practices are standard in the nursing home business. Second, it is not clear whether she has a responsibility to do anything about it. She does not work in the billing department, and her supervisor told her to stick to her own work. Should she invest time and effort into getting more information, risking a reprimand or worse if her supervisor finds out? And why should she go behind her supervisor's back? Doesn't she trust him? Doesn't she want him to trust her? It is very confusing.

In the classroom, ethical dilemmas are discussed and solutions deliberated in a nearly ideal setting. During the course of the semester, students get to know one another and a level of amiability and trust develops. If the class is well-managed, students are not afraid to share their deeply held convictions and, sometimes, their vulnerabilities with their professor and classmates. If everyone does not agree on how to resolve a difficult case, no matter. They move on to the next one. Even if a student disagrees with the professor, that's okay, as long as she backs up her position with sound reasoning.

But Lisa is not in the classroom. The situation she is facing is not hypothetical but real. And with reality comes strong emotions, like desire and fear: Lisa wants to believe her life amounts to something, that by doing her job well, she is helping people. She does not want to participate in fraud, but she does want to get along with the people with whom she works, especially her supervisor. She wants to earn his trust and respect. She does not want people to start treating her with suspicion. She definitely does not want to lose her job.

Will Lisa become cynical as the years pass? Many people do. Faced time and again with situations similar to Lisa's, they begin to feel that "business ethics" is an oxymoron. "Ethics is fine for the classroom," they might say, "but you quickly learn that work does not take place in an ivory tower. You adapt and survive and do what you have to do. That's what the real world demands."

But is that what the "real world" demands? Or is it just what some workplaces demand, while other employees, at other workplaces, find a much different set of behaviors and expectations?

This book contends that the range of possibilities for organizational life is vast, and that good workplaces, characterized by openness, trust, respect, and integrity, are not only possible but more likely to be healthy and successful.

If Lisa worked in such a place, and her supervisor was one of the people who sustained a culture of trust, she could ask questions about what she heard, they could talk about it, and then they could decide together what to do, if anything. This reveals a fundamental fact about ethical decision making in the workplace: it is fully effective only within the context of an already established ethical culture. In the absence of such a culture, ethical decision making is severely limited, because the open dialogue upon which it depends cannot take place.

This book is premised on the conviction that there are two broad types of ethical orientation especially relevant to the workplace. The first is *preventive*: it pays attention to building an ethical culture and establishing quality relationships among stakeholders in an organization, including executives, managers, employees, trustees, shareholders, customers, and community members. The second is *reactive*: it consists of figuring out what to do after things have gone wrong.

Reactive thinking is necessary, but necessarily limited. Sometimes there is no "good" thing to do. For example, the best thing for Humpty Dumpty is not to sit on the wall in the first place. After he tumbles from his precarious perch, there is no putting his shell back together again, no matter how well trained the king's men are in crisis management. Likewise, little is to be gained by trying to figure out "who is to blame" for a problem if there is no clear way to ensure it will not happen again. When something goes wrong in an organization, it is natural to react to the immediate need and ask, what should we do now? Nevertheless, for the long-term health of the organization, the more important question to ask is, what are the conditions that allowed this to happen?

Some would argue that the best way to establish an ethical culture is to develop a clear set of expectations, perhaps a code of ethics or values, a detailed list of policies explaining acceptable and unacceptable behavior, and a robust compliance program with people responsible for training and enforcing the policies.

But just as ethical decision making cannot stand on its own, neither can compliance. The central argument of this book is that a virtuous business culture creates the very conditions under which both ethical decision making and compliance can be effective. In an unethical business culture—a workplace characterized by fear, greed, distrust, manipulation, or dishonesty—genuine, sincere deliberation does not occur. That is perhaps obvious. But what is less obvious is that compliance is also undermined by an unethical culture. Codes, policies, and sanctions, after all, are just tools. In the right hands, they can be used positively and effectively. In the wrong hands, they can be destructive. It all comes down to who is using the tools, and why they are using them.

Consider, for example, a whistle-blowing program in a large corporation. In a healthy organization with reasonably high levels of trust and transparency, the program can be used to help identify individuals who are violating laws or codes of conduct. It can be the starting point for sincere investigations into allegations of wrongdoing that aim to make the organization better. But in a dysfunctional organization characterized by fear and distrust, whistle-blowing programs often serve to empower the wrongdoers. An employee witnesses a supervisor taking a bribe. She reports it through the whistle-blowing program. Weeks go by and she hears nothing back. An investigation may or may not be taking place, but information about it is not communicated. Meanwhile the supervisor's misconduct continues, and other employees observe and report it. Two more employees call the whistle-blower hotline. These employees talk to one another. The supervisor learns of the reports and begins taking revenge on the whistle-blowers—denying vacation requests, handing out disagreeable assignments, giving poor performance reviews. It seems the company cares more about protecting the supervisor than its employees. A sense of frustration and despair settles over the workplace.

Are whistle-blower programs important? Absolutely. This is especially true in large organizations where issues of accountability cannot be handled adequately in an immediate, face-to-face manner. But a whistle-blower program is not insurance against misconduct any more than a seat belt is insurance against injury. It has to be used, and used correctly, to be effective, but even then it can only function to reduce harm, not eliminate it.

This book is an attempt to take a big-picture look at the role of ethics in organizations. Its aim is not exhaustive; it does not try to cover all of the various sorts of ethical problems that can (and often do) arise in business settings. Rather, its aim is corrective, trying to redirect focus onto issues of culture first and problem solving second, demonstrating the many ways that good decision making depends upon the context of an ethical culture and also how good decision making, in turn, enhances and strengthens an ethical business culture. To this end, the first three chapters focus on ethical culture specifically, looking first at its basic components in chapter 1, the importance of ethical leadership in chapter 2, and relationships within healthy organizations in chapter 3. Chapter 4 describes a model for ethical decision making (the "Four-Way Method"). The use of that model is demonstrated in chapter 5, which includes a discussion of several case studies that provide an opportunity for addressing some of the persistent challenges facing those who endeavor to cultivate goodness.

Characteristics of organizational culture are best conveyed through stories. And so, distributed throughout the book are short stories of inspiring people who nurture and sustain an ethical culture in their organizations. For centuries, telling stories about good people has been the primary way of teaching ethics, because virtues, in the end, are grasped not by definition but through description, in stories told about the lives of the people who embody them.

CHAPTER 1

Growing Ethical Cultures

Lawn mowers and snowblowers are inherently dangerous. No matter how safe the Toro Company makes its machines, some people still get injured. Sometimes, they sue the manufacturer. The challenge for Toro is how to respond.

Generally speaking, deciding how to respond to lawsuits is considered a legal or financial matter, not a matter of ethics. After all, even if a company makes a dangerous product, as long as it incorporates the latest safety features, affixes the appropriate warning labels, and properly informs the customer about correct use of the product, it should not be held responsible for injuries. The company has every right to defend itself against lawsuits. The courts can decide where the fault lies. Anyway, that's the standard way of thinking.

But Toro does not think about injuries involving their products in the standard way. When Ken Melrose became CEO in 1983, he quickly went to work cultivating a new corporate culture focused on developing good relationships throughout the company, with management, employees, and customers. He envisioned a culture built on trust.

A culture of trust requires a willingness to admit fault, to share and collaborate to find solutions with mutual benefit. Lawsuits inevitably put people in adversarial positions; lawsuits create distrust by favoring solutions that have winners and losers. So Toro's product liability team came up with something called "alternate dispute resolution." Whenever someone was injured using one of the company's products, regardless of who might be at fault, they sent a team to investigate and—this is the crucial part—express remorse.

The remarkable thing about this story is that Toro's lawyers initiated the change. Here is how Ken Melrose describes it:

> In the early '90s, our product liability team thought the way we dealt with injured customers was inconsistent with our culture values. Though we were winning most of the cases, we still lost in effect, because of the financial costs and use of time and resources. Perhaps just as bad, we were treating the affected customers as the enemy. The legal team thought this was wrong, since our culture is about valuing people, both customers and employees.[1]

Toro went from an average of one hundred lawsuits a year, with half of them ending up in court, to settling two-thirds of their cases in-house and using a mediator for the rest. In the first fifteen years of the program, only one injury case went to court. In the first three years alone, Toro's liability insurance premium was reduced by $1.9 million.[2] Since that time, many other companies have followed Toro's lead and adopted mediation procedures for responding to liability issues. Many have done so because it makes good financial sense; others because it fit their culture; but few went as far as Toro in actively seeking out and establishing a relationship of goodwill with injured customers.

At the time Toro made the change, they did not know what would happen. They did it because it seemed like the right thing to do. And it seemed like the right thing to do because they had developed a culture that influenced people's perceptions of one another. Their customers went from being potential adversaries to neighbors.

This is part of what it means to develop an ethical culture: getting relationships right. That sounds simple, but it is actually

---

1. "Kendrick B. Melrose: Caring about People: Employees and Customers," *Ethix*, October 1, 2007, *http://ethix.org/2007/10/01/caring-about-people-employees-and-customers*. For the full story of Toro's culture change, see Kendrick B. Melrose, *Making the Grass Greener on Your Side: A CEO's Journey to Leading by Serving* (San Francisco: Berrett-Koehler Publishers, 1995).

2. Drew Mallick, "US Corporations Should Implement In-House Mediation Programs into Their Business Plans to Resolve Disputes," *Harvard Negotiation Law Review*, March 18, 2009, *http://www.hnlr.org/2009/03/us-corporations-should-implement-in-house-mediation-programs-into-their-business-plans-to-resolve-disputes/*.

extraordinarily difficult because people are complex beings, and organizations are complex arrangements of people.

The goal of the present chapter is to get a better understanding of what an ethical culture is. What does such a culture look like? Why is it important? What are its basic components or identifying features?

The Classical Virtues

A sensible place to start looking for the components of an ethical culture is in an organization's core values. After all, core values are intended to identify what a company stands for, what its most basic commitments are. And yet, it is surprising how many employees have difficulty naming their organization's core values. That is not necessarily due to a lapse of attention or memory on the part of the employees; rather it points to the fact that what leaders identify as their organization's "values" are frequently not grounded in the organization's character. Ask the same employees to describe the positive and negative traits of their organization—its virtues and vices—and they can readily tell you. For organizations, just as for individuals, there is often tension between how one acts and how one wants to be perceived.[3]

Consider the core values of the following organizations: Delta Airlines, Enron, Microsoft, and Verizon.

* Delta Airlines: honesty, integrity, respect, perseverance, servant leadership[4]
* Enron: respect, integrity, communication, excellence[5]
* Microsoft: integrity, honesty, passion, big challenges, open, respectful, accountable, self-critical[6]

---

3. See David Burkus, "A Tale of Two Cultures: Why Culture Trumps Core Values in Building Ethical Organizations," *Journal of Values Based Leadership* 4, no. 1 (Winter/Spring 2011), for a comparison of two very different corporate cultures: Enron and Zappos, *http://www.valuesbasedleadershipjournal.com/issues/vol4issue1/tale _2culture.php*.

4. Delta "Rules of the Road," *http://www.delta.com/content/dam/delta-www/pdfs /policy/delta-rules-of-the-road.pdf*.

5. Enron Code of Ethics, Enron (2000), *http://www.thesmokinggun.com/file/enrons -code-ethics*.

6. Microsoft, "Our Core Values," *https://www.microsoft.com/en-us/legal/compliance /buscond/overview.aspx*.

- Verizon: "We believe integrity is at the core of who we are. It establishes the trust that is critical to the relationships we have."[7]

Each organization emphasizes integrity as a value at the heart of its corporate culture. What precisely does that mean? Does it mean they all think integrity is a desirable characteristic of their organization? Does it mean they evaluate employees on the basis of integrity? Or does it mean that integrity accurately describes the character of their organization? Finally, does each organization even mean the same thing by the word "integrity"?

Such questions arise naturally as soon as one inquires into the nature of ethical culture and looks at the ways organizations typically try to define it for themselves. The difficulty in answering such questions reveals the severe limitations of the very idea of core values. This is not to say that value statements are meaningless; rather, they do not by themselves tell us very much about an organization.

To create and maintain an ethical culture, an organization must not only decide what it wishes to be (values), it must also take practical steps to make positive traits (virtues) a part of its everyday behavior and to root out negative traits (vices). And to do that, the leaders of an organization must know which traits are positive and which are negative. In other words, the leaders of an organization must know what makes a good (i.e., healthy, successful, or flourishing) organization. That is surprisingly difficult. There is no widely accepted definition of a "good" organization.

What if an organization has high earnings, but low employee engagement? Can an organization flourish if people do not like working there? On the other hand, if a company has high employee engagement but is on the verge of bankruptcy due to poor planning, would such a company be considered good? What if a company has high earnings and high engagement, but it manufactures something detrimental to the environment? In each of these cases, the organization may be said to lack integrity but for different reasons.

Consider the well-known children's story: *The Three Little Pigs.* The three pigs set out to make their way in the world, and each of

---

7. Verizon, "Who We Are," *http://www.verizon.com/jobs/verizon_credo.html.*

them decides to build a house. The first pig builds a house of straw, the second a house of sticks, and the third builds a house of bricks. A wolf comes along and huffs and puffs and blows down the houses of the first and second pigs, but he cannot destroy the brick house.

The story has been told to generations of children not just because (from the children's point of view) it is highly entertaining but also because (from the adults' point of view) it provides enduring lessons about character. What are those lessons?

The first two pigs come to a bad end because their efforts are slapdash; they lack foresight, persistence, and an ability to distinguish between needs and desires. The third pig, by contrast, possesses character traits that have long been valued in many different societies. First, he has *wisdom*, that is, he understands that his house may be needed to protect him from outside threats, so he makes it much stronger than it has to be during ordinary times. Second, he has *courage*, a strength of spirit demonstrated by his persistence in continuing to work on his house long after the other pigs have finished theirs and even, in some versions of the story, in spite of their ridicule. He is not afraid of appearing foolish. Third, he has *temperance*; that is, he invests his resources in the right things—the bricks needed to build a strong house and the time and effort to build it—which most likely requires him to forfeit some of the things he would otherwise like to have. The combination of these traits results in *integrity*, represented by the house itself: well-built, sturdy, able to withstand stress and strain. Integrity literally means "wholeness" or "strength," but in recent years, it has come to have a much broader range of meanings, quite similar to what used to be included under the classical virtue of *justice*.[8]

The four virtues of wisdom, courage, temperance, and justice are known as the "cardinal virtues." The earliest articulation of the cardinal virtues is found in Plato's *Republic*, and it arguably remains the best attempt to define goodness for individuals and groups. Plato tells of Socrates proposing that justice be thought of as a kind of harmony that results when a person or a society possesses wisdom,

---

8. Since in recent times the word "justice" has become associated almost exclusively with the realm of law and the courts, it is perhaps no surprise that another word (i.e., "integrity") took over its role of describing a life combining a multiplicity of virtues.

temperance, and courage. He claims that when all three virtues are present, and when wisdom leads the other two, then the fourth virtue, justice, naturally results.[9]

It is no accident that the idea of four cardinal virtues has persisted for 2,500 years and that we continue to find them expressed in various ways in cultures around the world. The cardinal virtues are grounded in an understanding of human nature as threefold: mind, body, and spirit. And even though values may vary greatly from one society or individual to the next, human nature remains essentially the same. That is, human beings are creatures who make decisions (mind), who desire (body), and who experience strong emotions like fear, anger, and pride (spirit). If you look around, you can see references to the three parts of human nature everywhere. Consider, for example, the YMCA logo.

© Ken Wolter / Shutterstock.com

The new YMCA logo incorporates a triangle representing mind, body, and spirit.

The logo, adopted in 2010, incorporates a triangle into the overall shape of a "Y." A press release explained the significance of the new design:

> The refreshed logo, with its multiple color options and new, contemporary look, better reflects the vibrancy of the Y and the diversity of the communities it serves. The new logo's bold, active and welcoming shape symbolizes the Y's commitment to personal and social progress.[10]

9. Plato, *Republic* 4.428a–435d, trans. G.M.A. Grube, rev. C.D.C. Reeve (Indianapolis: Hackett, 1992), 103–11.

10. The Y, "A Brand New Day: The YMCA Unveils New Brand Strategy to Further Community Impact," *http://www.ymca.net/news-releases/20100712-brand-new-day.html*.

There is no mention of why a triangle is featured in the design, but anyone familiar with the organization's history knows that a triangle has always been part of the YMCA image. That the triangle was intentionally chosen to symbolize the three components of a human being—mind, body, and spirit—and by inference their corresponding virtues, is evident in earlier versions of the logo.[11]

The L. Frank Baum novel, *The Wizard of Oz*, is another example of the pervasiveness of the cardinal virtues. The Scarecrow thinks he is foolish, the Tin Man thinks he has no feelings, and the Lion believes he is cowardly. Each believes he is deficient in mind, body, or spirit, but it turns out that they do in fact have those virtues, and working together, they succeed in rescuing Dorothy. They function as a team, demonstrating the integrity (wholeness or strength) of the three cardinal virtues working hand in hand. In the end, the Wizard acknowledges their strengths, revealing a significant insight about the virtues: they are more likely to be recognized by others than by the person who possesses them.

For more than two thousand years, in cultures all over the world, the cardinal virtues have been considered the key characteristics of a flourishing life—a life of wholeness, strength, and goodness—a life of integrity.

Organizational Hero
LOUISE HEMSTEAD

As chief operating officer for Organic Valley, a big part of Louise Hemstead's job is ensuring the quality and safety of their products. It's what keeps her awake at night and keeps her on the road throughout the year, meeting with members and partners all over the country.

Organic Valley is the largest organic, farmer-owned cooperative in North America. From a modest beginning in 1988 with

Continued

---

11. See "The History of the Y Logo," *http://www.ymca.net/sites/default/files/pdf/y-logo-history.pdf*.

just four family farms, the cooperative has grown to include 1,779 members. They sell dairy products, such as milk, cheese, and butter, as well as eggs, meat, and produce.

The consumer market for organic food has grown tremendously in recent years, mainly due to concerns about the safety and nutritional value of traditionally farmed products. Organic certification requires products to be grown without the use of synthetic fertilizers, hormones, herbicides, or pesticides. But customers also expect more. They expect the "organic" label to mean assurance of safety for every product throughout the farm-to-table journey. That is why Organic Valley goes to great lengths to ensure that all dairy products are safe, passing fifty-seven points of inspection in a program overseen by twenty-five full-time employees dedicated to quality assurance.

But quality assurance at Organic Valley began with just one person: Louise Hemstead. In 1993, Louise and her husband, David, owned a small dairy farm just down the road from the newly formed co-op. With two young children at home, the twenty-five cow farm was not enough to support their family, so Louise applied for a position as the dairy program coordinator at Organic Valley. She became the co-op's first dairy professional.

One of her early tasks was to test products for contaminants. She discovered that 35 percent of the cheese tested positive for *E coli*, a bacteria that can cause serious health problems. At that time, Organic Valley was a pioneer in the field of organic dairy, and there were few industry standards. Little was known about the potential seriousness of bacterial contamination. When she reported the results to her superiors, they told her not to worry about it. After all, they reasoned, hadn't they sold the same cheese the week before without anybody getting sick? But Louise was insistent: "Either the cheese goes, or I go."

She left work that evening not knowing what her bosses would decide to do. Halfway home, she pulled off onto the side

Continued

Organizational Hero: LOUISE HEMSTEAD *Continued*

of the road, tears in her eyes. She reflected on what she had done. Would she still have a job in the morning? How would she and her husband support their young family?

The next morning, she returned to work to find that Organic Valley had decided to get rid of the contaminated inventory. "That was a huge hardship for the co-op," Louise said. "Harder than I knew at the time. We were barely surviving. But it was the right thing to do."

Companies, just like people, grow through a maturing process, and early decisions set the stage for future growth. The stand Louise took on contaminated cheese was the first step in establishing a corporate culture dedicated to safety and quality. But it also was a crucial step in Louise's professional growth, earning her respect throughout the company as a person of integrity.

The Limits of Compliance

One may be inclined to think that there are ways to ensure integrity without appealing to character. If only one puts into place the right rules and policies, and then provides training along with relevant sanctions and incentives, good behavior will result. To some extent, that is true. A good compliance framework—that is, a set of policies or standards that communicate an organization's expectations, training programs that serve to remind people what the standards are and also establish a common vocabulary for ethical behavior, and effective instruments for assessing whether members of an organization are abiding by the standards—can be very important. That is especially so in large organizations where informal means of communication cannot be relied upon to establish and maintain a shared vision of the group's expectations.

But codes, rules, policies, and standards are no substitute for character. They only address people's behavior, not their motivations. And there is no way to anticipate in advance all the ways a person should act to do what is good, or all the ways a person must refrain from acting in order to avoid doing harm. The more one tries to be detailed and exhaustive in specifying desired and undesired behaviors, the more likely one is to unintentionally discourage some significant good behaviors and encourage some bad behaviors. In an organization comprised of many people with questionable character, a strong compliance program may be helpful to keep people "in line" and to keep really bad things from happening. But in an organization comprised of virtuous people, a strong compliance framework is more likely to hold an organization back, to keep it from reaching its ethical potential.

To understand why this is so, consider the example of a hospital janitor who was interviewed about her job as part of a research study: "Charlayne told [the researchers] about how she ignored her supervisor's admonitions and refrained from vacuuming the visitors' lounge while some family members, who were there all day, every day, happened to be napping."[12]

Charlayne did the right thing, even though it was contrary to policy, because she understood that the mission of the hospital was to care for patients and that caring for family members of patients went along with that mission. She had a proper understanding of her role in relation to the mission (wisdom), and she was not afraid to go against her supervisor's instructions in order to do the right thing (courage).

At the university where I work, a custodian named Wayne came into a classroom one day and handed a student a bottle of soda. As he did so, he said, "Thank you for telling me about the spill so I could get it cleaned up quickly." When asked about it later, he explained,

> The student dropped an open bottle of soda on the stairwell, and it sprayed all over the walls and steps down two flights of stairs. He found me right away and told me what happened, and I could tell he felt really bad about it. So after cleaning up the stairs, I went over to the vending machines and bought him a new one. I just wanted to let him know I wasn't upset.

---

12. Barry Schwartz and Kenneth Sharpe, *Practical Wisdom: The Right Way to Do the Right Thing* (New York: Riverhead Books, 2010), 16.

There is nothing in Wayne's job description that requires him to be generous to others, to go out of his way to make the people he interacts with feel better, but he did these things anyway. His wisdom led him to understand that the action was important; his temperance led him to do it even though he had to pay for the soda out of his own pocket.

The interesting thing about these examples is that the people in them do the right thing not because of the rules but despite the rules, which means they have some other way of determining what should be done in a particular situation. They think broadly about organizational purpose, and then they think about how best to accomplish that purpose given their role within the organization and the tools at their disposal. In other words, they use practical wisdom.

Traditional ethics programs that emphasize compliance often don't work, or at least they don't work as well as intended, because they tend to be too narrowly focused on precisely *how* things should be done (rules and policies) instead of *why* something should be done (purpose). Training that focuses on organizational values tends to be more successful, probably because values are often explicitly or implicitly connected to purpose, but still the desired effect of promoting more ethical behavior tends to be short-lived.[13]

Why doesn't ethics training lead to lasting improvement? To begin to understand the answer, the question must be put in the context of a much larger one: why do people—even basically good people—do bad things?

One of the earliest philosophical explorations of this question comes from Saint Augustine. In his *Confessions*, he asks, Do people ever do bad things for no good reason at all, just because they want to do something bad? Augustine considers a number of examples, including a story from his own childhood when he and some other kids stole pears from an orchard.

> There was a pear tree near our vineyard, heavy with fruit,
> but fruit that was not particularly tempting either to look
> at or to taste. A group of young blackguards, and I among

---

13. See Danielle E. Warren, Joseph Gaspar, and William S. Laufer, "Is Formal Ethics Training Merely Cosmetic? A Study of Ethics Training and Ethical Organizational Culture," *Business Ethics Quarterly* 24, no. 1 (2014): 85–117.

them, went out to knock down the pears and carry them off late one night, for it was our bad habit to carry on our games in the streets till very late. We carried off an immense load of pears, not to eat—for we barely tasted them before throwing them to the hogs. Our only pleasure in doing it was that it was forbidden.[14]

Surely, Augustine thought, that is a case in which he did something just because it was wrong, and for no other reason: "I had any number of better pears of my own, and plucked those only that I might steal."[15] But then he reconsiders: even though he did not want the pears themselves, perhaps there was some other motive. "Now—as I think back on the state of my mind then—I am altogether certain that I would not have done it alone. Perhaps then what I really loved was the companionship of those with whom I did it. If so, can I still say that I loved nothing over and above the thievery?"[16]

Augustine concludes that he stole the pears because he wanted to earn the esteem of the other kids. He valued friendship. That, in itself, is a good thing, but not when it comes at the cost of doing harm to someone else.

In the end, Augustine answers his original question: people always do what they think is "good" (in some respect) at the time. People may very well know that their action is against the law, or against societal custom, or against another person's wishes, but they will always have some positive reason, something they want to accomplish through their actions.

Augustine concludes that the reason people do bad things is not because they want something bad to happen; rather, they do them because it seems at the time to be "good" in some respect, even if they know it is against the law or contrary to moral standards. After all, in stealing the pears he did something that he knew was considered to be "wrong," but, at the same time, it seemed to him like a good thing. It seemed like a means to achieving something worthwhile, namely friendship.

---

14. Augustine, *Confessions* 2.4, trans. F.J. Sheed (Indianapolis: Hackett, 1993).
15. Ibid., 6.28.
16. Ibid., 8.30.

This leads Augustine to reflect that the source of all wrong-doing, deeply ingrained in human nature, is ignorance. Such ignorance takes three forms.

- The first form of ignorance is unintentional, as when one does not know what the right thing to do is or happens to be ignorant of the negative effects of his or her actions upon someone else. An example would be the owner of a small business who requires employees to buy their own uniforms, not realizing the significant financial burden he or she is placing upon some of them in the first few weeks of a new job.

- The second is willful ignorance, also known as self-deception. An example is when one purposefully directs one's attention away from certain features of a situation. In Augustine's story about stealing the pears, he does not think about how the loss of the fruit may affect the owner of the pear tree; his attention is directed elsewhere, toward what his companions think about him.

- The third type of ignorance is misplaced desire. Sometimes, one wants the wrong sort of things, things that may be harmful to oneself, or things that may be good in some narrow sense but not in a broader sense. A toddler may reach for a cup on the table, not knowing that he really would not like hot coffee. A mid-level manager may want a promotion, not realizing that the increased stress that the new job brings will make her miserable. In Augustine's example, he discovered that while it is good to have friends, the bonds formed by trying to impress some by harming others do not constitute genuine friendship, and they eventually prove illusory.

The three types of ignorance are not exclusive. Indeed, they frequently complement and reinforce one another. Consider a recent op-ed piece from a former Wall Street trader, Sam Polk. He explains why he gave up his profession, despite earning more than he had ever dreamed was possible by the age of thirty:

> I wanted a billion dollars. It's staggering to think that in the course of five years, I'd gone from being thrilled at my first bonus—$40,000—to being disappointed when, my second

year at the hedge fund, I was paid "only" $1.5 million. But, in the end, it was actually my absurdly wealthy bosses who helped me see the limitations of unlimited wealth. I was in a meeting with one of them, and a few other traders, and they were talking about the new hedge-fund regulations. Most everyone on Wall Street thought they were a bad idea. "But isn't it better for the system as a whole?" I asked. The room went quiet, and my boss shot me a withering look. I remember his saying, "I don't have the brain capacity to think about the system as a whole. All I'm concerned with is how this affects our company." I felt as if I'd been punched in the gut. He was afraid of losing money, despite all that he had.[17]

Polk likens the greed of his fellow traders to drug addicts who will do anything to get a fix. Their misplaced desire for fantastic sums of money leads to fear of losing their wealth and a very narrow focus on what is good for them individually to the exclusion of all others. Greed leads to cowardice, which leads to ignorance. And the result, concludes Polk, is a financial system without integrity.

I'd always looked enviously at the people who earned more than I did; now, for the first time, I was embarrassed for them, and for me. I made in a single year more than my mom made her whole life. I knew that wasn't fair; that wasn't right. Yes, I was sharp, good with numbers. I had marketable talents. But in the end I didn't really do anything. I was a derivatives trader, and it occurred to me the world would hardly change at all if credit derivatives ceased to exist. Not so nurse practitioners. What had seemed normal now seemed deeply distorted.[18]

When people are under the influence of a "deeply distorted" picture of themselves and the world in which they live, their choices inevitably exhibit the qualities of injustice. It is not that they are purposefully making "bad" choices, but neither is there a sound context

---

17. "For the Love of Money," *New York Times*, January 18, 2014.
18. Ibid.

for making "good" choices. In such a situation, it may be difficult to address questions of ethics in a straightforward fashion. Simple statements of core values, rules, and policies may be effective guides to ethical choices when the people who are using them already possess good character. Such an approach to corporate ethics may effectively address problems caused by unintentional ignorance by providing basic reminders of what to do or how to do it. In order to counteract misplaced desire, an organization may need to go further, implementing a strong compliance program consisting of incentives for good conduct and sanctions for improper conduct. But even that will do very little to address the deeper forms of moral disengagement that come from self-deception and grossly misplaced desire. To do that, an organization must focus on the development of good character. Indeed, without good character as a starting point, well-intentioned attempts to motivate good behavior may even be counterproductive.

Recent research on the effectiveness of financial incentives to encourage better behavior challenges the seemingly commonsense assumption that the more you reward people, the more likely they are to engage in ethical behavior. Here is how Barry Schwartz sums up a few of the studies:

> Swiss economists Bruno Frey (University of Zurich) and Felix Oberholzer-Gee (Harvard Business School) have shown that when Swiss citizens are offered a substantial cash incentive for agreeing to have a toxic waste dump in their community, their willingness to accept the facility falls by half. Uri Gneezy (U.C. San Diego's Rady School of Management) and Aldo Rustichini (University of Minnesota) observed that when Israeli day-care centers fine parents who pick up their kids late, lateness increases. And James Heyman (University of St. Thomas) and Dan Ariely (Duke's Fuqua School of Business) showed that when people offer passers-by a token payment for help lifting a couch from a van, they are less likely to lend a hand than if they are offered nothing.[19]

---

19. "The Dark Side of Incentives," *Bloomberg Businessweek Magazine*, November 12, 2009, *http://www.bloomberg.com/bw/magazine/content/09_47/b4156084807874.htm*.

The reason financial incentives often fail to work the way they are intended is that they do not enhance altruistic motivation; instead, they compete with it. Instead of giving support, for example, to a person's prosocial impulse to help another, they appeal to the person's self-interest. And if the self-interest motivation isn't sufficient to generate the desired behavior, the person is less likely to do it than without the incentive.

James Heyman and Dan Ariely explain this by suggesting there are really two types of markets: monetary and social.[20] If businesses try to encourage employees to do what is right by offering a financial incentive, they may unintentionally undermine the social motivation that already is in place. In short, if you begin with the assumption that most people are basically selfish, cowardly, and foolish, and provide incentives for them to do the right thing based on that assumption, they are more likely to respond as if they actually are that way. The assumption becomes self-fulfilling.

To repeat, integrity is the virtue of wholeness and strength. It can only be maintained in the presence of wisdom, which addresses ignorance; courage, which addresses fear; and temperance, which addresses misplaced desire. These are the necessary conditions of integrity. One could think of them as the three legs of a stool. Remove any one of them and the stool cannot stay upright. Ignorance, fear, and greed can undermine even the most thorough ethical framework.

In hindsight, this can seem obvious. On July 1, 2000, Ken Lay, CEO of Enron, sent a memo to all employees describing the corporation's core values. At the time, the Houston, Texas–based energy company was widely regarded as one of America's most successful companies, with more than $100 billion in annual revenue and twenty thousand employees. Eighteen months later, the company declared bankruptcy. And while Enron's growth and subsequent collapse were chiefly due to an intentional scheme of fraudulent accounting practices designed and perpetrated by the company's

---

20. James Heyman and Dan Ariely, "Effort for Payment: A Tale of Two Markets," *Psychological Science* 15, no. 11 (2004): 787–93. Also see Tim Kasser, *The High Price of Materialism* (Cambridge, MA: MIT Press, 2003), for an account of the two basic types of motivation: intrinsic and extrinsic. People motivated by intrinsic values (e.g., the common good) tend to be happier, healthier, and less insecure than people motivated by extrinsic values (money or prestige).

executive officers, the fraud would not have been nearly as successful for so long without the widespread cultivation of a corporate culture that managed to deceive and manipulate investors, government regulators, politicians, employees, and the press.

Much has been made of the vast amount of intelligence that went into building the Enron empire. A best-selling book, *The Smartest Guys in the Room*, was even written about the scandal.[21] But being smart is not the same as being wise, and Enron's culture of deception and miscommunication undermined the very conditions in which wisdom—a genuine understanding of what is happening and why it is or is not important—thrives. Furthermore, Enron's corporate leaders had intentionally set up their hiring and promotion process based upon the misguided notion that people are effectively motivated by greed and fear:

> Enron followed [McKinsey & Company's] advice almost to the letter, setting up internal performance review committees. The members got together twice a year, and graded each person in their section on ten separate criteria, using a scale of one to five. The process was called "rank and yank." Those graded at the top of their unit received bonuses two-thirds higher than those in the next thirty per cent; those who ranked at the bottom received no bonuses and no extra stock options—and in some cases were pushed out.[22]

When a corporate culture is built on the basis of ignorance, greed, and fear, it not only allows for but actively cultivates moral disengagement. Is it any wonder such an organization fails?

Many people in leadership positions operate under the false assumption that a majority of people dislike work, and therefore one must use either sanctions (threats, punishments) or incentives (bonuses, rewards) or both to get them to do it. Social psychologist Douglas McGregor termed this notion "Theory X."[23] It is

---

21. Bethany McLean and Peter Elkind, *The Smartest Guys in the Room* (New York: Portfolio, 2004).

22. Malcolm Gladwell, "The Talent Myth," *New Yorker*, July 22, 2002, *http://www.newyorker.com/magazine/2002/07/22/the-talent-myth*.

23. *The Human Side of Enterprise* (New York: McGraw-Hill, 1960).

the basis for the "carrot and stick" approach to management. And while it may be true of some people, the fact is that most people like to work, provided that they find the work meaningful and the working conditions decent. McGregor termed this latter notion "Theory Y." He believed that people generally want to be treated with respect, to be given responsibility, and to be appreciated for the work they do.[24]

Peter F. Drucker argued that both theories have merit. Sometimes people have to be pushed or prodded to do their work competently and thoroughly, but most also want to achieve something worthwhile in the workplace. And so the wise leader, understanding that human motivation is complex, will acknowledge the need for a compliance framework (sanctions and incentives) on the one hand, and a culture of character (goodness and meaning) on the other. Both approaches are necessary.

Fortunately, there are many resources available on how to develop a compliance framework. Developing a culture of character is much harder, partly because less attention has been paid to how to do it well and it takes more patience and skill. In short, how can one get people in an organization to do what Charlayne, and Wayne, and the legal team at Toro did: to actively seek to be fully, morally engaged?

Communities of Character

Think about the last time you faced a significant ethical problem. Perhaps you observed questionable behavior on the part of someone with whom you work. Perhaps somebody falsely accused you of wrongdoing, and you had to decide how to respond. Perhaps you had to make a decision that would be technically against the rules but would be a considerable help to someone else. How did you figure out what to do?

If you are like most people, you talked to someone with experience and good judgment, someone who is a good listener. That is because most people seek advice from people they trust. This is

---

24. For a thorough discussion of Theories X and Y, see Peter F. Drucker, *Management: Tasks, Responsibilities, Practices* (New York: Harper & Row, 1973), 231–45.

common sense. When one encounters a difficult problem, one typically seeks help from friends and acquaintances who are willing and able to help. The people most willing and able to help with ethical problems are people of integrity, people one counts on because one knows their judgment is not corrupted by personal interests, swayed by strong emotion, or distracted by an inability to pay attention. And yet few leaders of organizations recognize that one of the most important things they can do to create a more ethical workplace is to encourage more trusting relationships. In such an environment, constructive conversations about how to do the right thing seem to flow naturally. Trust flourishes in a community of character.

Just as people have distinct character traits—sets of virtues and vices that define them—so do organizations. And just as with a person, an organization's character sometimes may be immediately evident. Consider the following:

In store A, the employees smile and greet each customer in a friendly manner. Laughter and jokes can be heard. One can tell people enjoy working there. If there is trouble finding an item, a clerk walks customers over to a coworker who knows just what is needed. It is a pleasure to shop in that place.

In store B, the experience is quite different. The employees don't make eye contact. Nobody asks customers if they need help. Everyone is busy, but they are completely engaged in their separate tasks; they are not interacting with one another. Upon checking out, the cashier asks each customer, "Did you find everything you were looking for?" But it is obviously not a genuine inquiry. It is just something management requires her to say.

From initial impressions, one would be justified in thinking that store A is more likely to be an ethical workplace than store B. It is not just that store A provides a better shopping experience for the customer. In store A the employees are more likely to talk to one another about how to handle difficult problems when they arise. More importantly, they are more likely to anticipate problems and address them together effectively before they become serious ethical issues.

How does a workplace become a good place to work? One contributing factor is that people of good character are hired, retained, and promoted. People of poor character are not. The business author

Jim Collins refers to this as "getting the right people on the bus."[25] One cannot hire selfish, lazy, envious, cowardly people and expect them to contribute to a positive workplace atmosphere. Wise organizations pay close attention to the character of the people they hire.

But that is not the only factor. Most people are neither extremely virtuous nor extremely vicious; they fall somewhere in the middle. As a consequence, their immediate environment has a great deal of influence on how they act and, especially, on how they interact with others. That is why another key factor in positive workplaces is that people are united by a shared purpose. They may not all be able to articulate fully what that purpose is, and they may disagree, at times, about how best to achieve that purpose, but it shapes their common identity. It determines how they think of themselves and how they feel about the time they spend together.

Saint Augustine famously defined a "people" as those bound together by what they love in common.[26] To be a community (or a "people") it is not enough simply to be in the same place at the same time. That can happen by accident. Nor is it enough for everyone to be doing the same thing. That could describe a group of people fighting one another over possession of some piece of property. To be a community takes some common purpose or goal—something they all want together, something they believe to be, in some sense, greater than themselves, worthy of sacrifice. Most people are willing to put a great deal of time and effort into things they believe are important and little time or effort into things they believe to be pointless.

Not all organizations constitute communities. Different kinds of organizations are established for different purposes, and people join organizations for a number of reasons. The chief purpose of most businesses, for example, is to make a profit, and one of the main reasons people work in businesses is to earn a living. But to be a community there must also be a shared purpose that unites people in pursuit of something they all regard as worthwhile, something that goes beyond whatever personal reasons they might have for being involved.

---

25. *Good to Great: Why Some Companies Make the Leap . . . and Others Don't* (New York: HarperBusiness, 2001), 41–64.

26. Augustine, *City of God* 9.24.

Nobody knows more about the dynamics of community building than Jean Vanier, founder of L'Arche:

> Community takes a long time to form. It takes a long time for barriers to drop, for mutual confidence to grow, for nonverbal communication to become more important than words. A community is only a community when most of the people in it have made the passage from "the community for me" to "me for the community." A community is only a community when most of the people in it are conscientiously trying to seek the fulfillment, peace and happiness of every other member of it.[27]

What is it that the people who work at store A love in common? To what are they all committed? It could be any number of things. It could be that they believe deeply in the goodness of the product or service they are offering; it could be that they care about one another and are committed to the betterment of one another's lives; it could be that they understand the role their business serves in the community and know that if they do well the whole community benefits.

Whatever the commitment is, it will be apparent when members of the organization are asked to tell their deep story.[28] The deep story is the narrative that reveals the heart of the organization and allows each member of it to find their place. Because every organization is made up of individuals who usually enter at different times in the organization's history and bring to the place their own interests, concerns, desires, and perceptions, each one needs to discover how he or she fits into the culture. The deep story allows them to do this in a deliberate and meaningful way. If the deep story is not told on a regular basis, and if each member is not allowed the opportunity to find his or her own place within the story, even the most successfully integrated organizations that have succeeded in progressing from a collection of "I's" into a unified "we" will gradually disintegrate and

---

27. Jean Vanier, *Be Not Afraid* (New York: Paulist Press, 1975), 78.

28. The idea of the "deep story" comes from John Haughey, SJ, of the Woodstock Theological Center at Georgetown University. The way I am using the notion here is indebted to Father Haughey's writings, but any misapplication of it is strictly my own doing. For those interested in learning more, please see *Converting Nine to Five: Bringing Spirituality to Your Daily Work* (New York: Crossroad, 1989).

fragment into a collection of "I's" once again. They will become a group of individuals, inhabiting the same place at the same time, doing similar kinds of things, but they will not be a community.

Tom Chappell, the founder of Tom's of Maine, a producer of all-natural personal care products, believes in the significance of storytelling as a way of bringing his employees together into a cohesive organization. In *The Soul of a Business*, he tells the company's deep story, about how he and his wife Kate started the company together with a $5,000 loan and a plan to manufacture and sell an environmentally friendly, phosphate-free laundry detergent. As they grew and developed new products, they made a pledge not to conduct any animal testing, even though it was required at the time by the Food and Drug Administration. They stuck to their guns, which resulted in a lawsuit with the federal government. They eventually prevailed, though not without a great deal of financial hardship and uncertainty, including the real possibility that they would lose the company altogether. Difficult times like that tend to unify those who go through them. A strong community is formed, and the challenge becomes how to bring new employees into an already established community. Chappell's story is significant because it reveals his awareness that successfully going through a crisis together is both a blessing and a curse. He understands that storytelling is not just about what happened in the past, but a matter of connecting the past to the present and the present to the future.

> The employees at Tom's of Maine come from all walks of life. Workers making $30,000 a year are bound to view things differently from executives who arrive at Tom's from a Fortune 500 company. What does the Mission mean to eighty-five different people? The only way I can find out is if I try to get to know those people, if I listen to their stories, which will reveal the symbols—the meaning—of their lives. Storytelling can be an effective teaching tool because learning is not limited to what goes on in your mind. It is also about sharing what you know with others, and they with you. We all have our own beliefs, but we cannot expect others to understand who we really are if we keep those beliefs to ourselves.[29]

---

29. Tom Chappell, *The Soul of a Business* (New York: Bantam Books, 1993), 71.

When people regularly have the opportunity to tell their stories, they not only share a part of themselves, they discover a new and more expansive identity as they find their individual story woven together with others' stories into the deep story of the organization. A genuine commitment to ethics comes from here. It is a substantial, personal commitment to do the right thing because one cares about what happens to these people, in this place.

Organizational Hero
SUE MARVIN

When the subprime mortgage industry collapsed in 2007, it created a ripple effect throughout the US economy. Businesses in the construction industry were hit hardest. By 2009, companies making supplies for new housing were closing factories and laying off employees. An exception was Marvin Windows and Doors of Warroad, Minnesota.

The recession hit Marvin Windows just as hard as other manufacturers. Orders for new construction fell by two-thirds. Like everyone else in the housing industry at the time, company executives had to find ways to cut costs. Laying off employees was deemed out of the question, however.

The company's president, Sue Marvin, is the granddaughter of founder George Griffin Marvin. In an interview on Minnesota Public Radio, she recalled the meeting in which the family first shaped a long-term plan for dealing with the crisis.

> I sat down with my two brothers—Jake, who is our CEO, and George, who is in charge of all our plants. And we said, "Okay, we've got to cut expenses, and we've got to do it quickly. What do we do?" So, we didn't consider cutting our workforce, because we have always said, "Our employees are our greatest asset." . . . It was, we will immediately do whatever we can to make it through this recession without a layoff. We wouldn't put

Continued

Organizational Hero: SUE MARVIN *Continued*

the company at risk. I mean if it came down to staying in business or not, then we would do what we would have to do, but, it was, we will do everything else first. And, if we can continue to serve our customers, and continue the health of the business without laying off an employee, then that is what we're going to do. So, we looked for other ways to cut expenses.[30]

They cut wages by 5 percent. They reduced hours from forty to thirty-two hours per week and eliminated overtime. They cut benefits like 401k contributions, tuition reimbursement, and profit sharing, but they maintained employee health insurance. Gradually, as the housing market recovered and new construction increased, they were able to increase hours and restore benefits, but it took a long time.

One reason they were able to make the decision to keep employees working is that Marvin Windows is a family-owned, private company. They did not have pressure, as many publicly held companies do, to make decisions based on quarterly earnings reports. They had the option of making long-term plans, and their plans paid off. During the recession, none of the owners took any profits from the company, and now the company is benefitting from increased customer loyalty and a considerable market share gained from their competitors.

The decision to invest in their employees was not just a business decision; it was an ethical decision, based in the company's values. To understand the company's decision, one must know something about Marvin Windows' deep story.

In the nearly one hundred years since George Griffin Marvin founded the company, Marvin Windows and the small town of Warroad practically grew up together. The population of Warroad is 1,773. Of Marvin Window's 4,300 employees, 2,000 of them

Continued

---

30. "The State of Minnesota Business Ethics," *Minnesota Public Radio*, November 19, 2014, *http://www.mprnews.org/story/2014/11/19/daily-circuit-business-ethics.*

Organizational Hero: SUE MARVIN *Continued*

work in the Warroad factory. The town and company have been through crises before.

In 1961, fire destroyed the factory and all of its machinery. Afterward, the family gathered to talk about what to do. Should they rebuild or walk away? Jake recalls hearing his uncle declare, "My God, this is home. I'm staying here if I have to dig ditches to make a living." George, nearly eighty years old at the time, agreed: "We'll start tomorrow," he said, "and we'll make it bigger and better."[31]

Stories like this one ground the company's third- and fourth-generation leaders in a history of making important decisions based on the company's values, and give them a sense of purpose as they look toward the future. Reflecting on that future, Sue Marvin observed, "This company could become very much like the way the world sees European companies where you talk about the transfer of the company not from generation to generation but from century to century."[32]

Father John Haughey, the author of several books on organizational ethics, explains the role of stories in shaping an ethical culture:

It seems to me that the primary ethical issue with all of us . . . is the issue of personal identity: the key here is to see that each of us is a part of many stories. . . . Of these stories of which I am a part, which is my organizing story? And what effect is this organizing story having on me? Is it a comprehensive account of the true and the good as my conscience and mind understand these? Does it unify my life and give it meaning?[33]

---

31. "Marvin Windows and Doors 100 Years of Marvin History," *https://www .youtube.com/watch?v=KIoiXOrzl8A.*

32. Ibid.

33. John C. Haughey, "Enhancing the Traditions," *Conversations on Jesuit Higher Education* 22, no. 8 (2002): 34.

Recall the opening story about what happened at Toro. The legal team came to the CEO with a proposal to change how they handled product liability cases because everyone else in the company had bought into the idea that valuing people was part of their common identity. They wanted to be part of that common identity also. They wanted to be integrated into the deep story. And that required them to stop treating the customer as the enemy.

Conclusion

Max De Pree, former CEO of Herman Miller, a Michigan-based furniture company, asserts, "Leadership is a serious meddling in other people's lives."[34] He could say that because he understood that organizations have a profound influence on the people who work in them—not just on what they do but on who they are, how they see their relationships to others, how they tell the story of their lives. Each story is interwoven with the stories of coworkers, true, but it is also interwoven with the stories of parents, spouses, children, neighbors, and friends. To take ethics in an organization seriously is to see the organization as a community within communities. It is also to acknowledge that communities both take on the character of the people within them and help shape the character of those people as well.

Character is reflected not only in how we act but in how we talk to and about one another. Basketball teams that do not communicate on the floor have losing records. Surgical teams that do not talk with each other have more negative outcomes. Sales people who are constantly arguing with each other provide lousy customer service.

When our talk is focused on the common good, when the good for all of us and not just for individuals becomes central to the stories we tell, we start to become more attuned to the possibilities for positive interaction with others on a daily basis. Our very picture of what it means to live a successful, flourishing life changes—not immediately, of course, but gradually, almost imperceptibly, day by day.

---

34. Max DePree, "The Leadership Quest: Three Things Necessary," *Business Strategy Review* 4, no. 1 (1993): 69.

An organization with an ethical culture will necessarily possess integrity, and it will be recognized by three defining characteristics:

1. It will be a *wise* culture: people will care about what they are doing and about one another, so they will talk together, continually trying to figure out how things can be done better.

2. It will be a *temperate* culture: people in the organization will care about the long-term health of the whole, so they will not squander resources or look for short-term solutions that are likely to cause problems down the road.

3. It will be a *courageous* culture: people in the organization will not be afraid to speak up, and they will encourage one another to take a stand for what is right.

This does not mean that an ethical organizational culture, a community of character, obviates the need for ethical rules, policies, standards, and training. Rather, an ethical culture establishes the necessary context within which a framework of compliance can reasonably be expected to function as intended. In such a context, and only within such a context, can members of an organization work together to create and maintain some measure of mutual accountability by means of which they all may flourish.

Discussion Questions

1. Can you think of any organizations with an ethical culture? What makes them stand apart from others?

2. In addition to the four classical virtues of wisdom, courage, temperance, and justice, what are other important virtues for organizations to cultivate?

3. Think of the organizations with which you are familiar. Do people in the organizations trust one another? What are some practical steps organizations can take to enhance the level of trust?

4. What is the "deep story" of your university or of a place where you work?

Resources for Further Exploration ——————

PRINT

Collins, Jim. *Good to Great: Why Some Companies Make the Leap . . . and Others Don't.* New York: HarperBusiness, 2001.

> This well-known book is a great resource, primarily for its description of the character traits that comprise the leaders of top-performing companies.

Plato. *The Republic.* Translated by G.M.A. Grube. Revised by C.D.C. Reeve. Indianapolis: Hackett, 1992.

> The first articulation of what came later to be known as the "cardinal virtues" occurs in Plato's *Republic.* This book is invaluable for the student of business ethics for its discussion of how injustice arises in society and the relationship between character in individuals and in communities.

OTHER MEDIA

Gibney, Alex, et al. *Enron: The Smartest Guys in the Room.* DVD. Los Angeles: Magnolia Home Entertainment, 2005. Time: 01:50:00.

> For a vivid portrayal of the character traits that destroy organizations, this documentary by Alex Gibney is hard to beat. It is based on the book of the same title by Bethany MacLean and Peter Elkind.

Schwarz, Barry. "Using Our Practical Wisdom." TED video. Time: 00:23:07. *http://www.ted.com/talks/barry_schwartz_using_our_practical_wisdom.*

> This video lecture by psychologist Barry Schwarz is a useful supplement to any discussion of the role of wisdom in ethical decision making.

CHAPTER 2

Ethical Leadership

In the 1957 movie *Desk Set,* Spencer Tracy plays Richard Sumner, an absentminded efficiency expert hired to streamline operations in the reference department of a television network. Katherine Hepburn plays Bunny Watson, supervisor of the department, who is concerned that Sumner intends to replace her staff with an "electronic brain," a large computer named EMERAC.

The movie, ostensibly a romantic comedy, depicted a genuine threat felt by many workers during the industrial automation of the mid-twentieth century, especially as the rapid development of computer technology promised, for the first time, to take over many tasks routinely performed by office workers.

The movie winds up happily for the office staff, but only because EMERAC mistakenly sends "pink slips" to every employee of the company, including the head of the network, thus demonstrating the indispensability of people to keep operations going smoothly. Computers, like machines in general, may assist human beings but can never replace them, the movie seems to say. And yet the movie supplies more questions than answers. Does friendship enhance the workplace, or is it merely a distraction? Is productivity the only measure of human worth? And, most significantly, what if EMERAC had performed flawlessly?

That last question is never taken up by the movie, perhaps because it does not really matter to the central plot. The real drama of *Desk Set* is driven by the growing romantic attachment between Sumner and Watson, two people who seem at first to be completely at odds, not only because Sumner's computer threatens to displace Watson's staff, but because Sumner is a stereotypical engineer, committed to science and progress, more comfortable in the neat and predictable world of machines than in the messy turmoil of human interactions. Watson, by contrast, is fond of literature and the arts; she likes living things, and tends a philodendron whose vines wrap around all four walls of her office; she thrives under conditions of chaos and confusion. Although she has a long-standing romantic relationship with Mike Cutler, a manager at the network, at the end of the movie she rejects Cutler in favor of Sumner. Sumner is honest and forthright with her. He listens to her attentively; he values her opinions; he treats her like a person.

The movie suggests that the real threat of the modern, highly efficient bureaucratic workplace may not be that machines are replacing people, but rather that people are often treated like machines. This raises a significant ethical question for anyone who works in an organization, especially for those who have significant leadership roles. What does it mean to treat a person with dignity and respect and not as a thing? And why is that important?

The Hawthorne Studies

Human beings and machines have long had an uneasy coexistence in the workplace. Machines can be designed to make work easier, more productive, and to reduce or eliminate some of the less desirable, mind-numbing tasks necessary to keep businesses operating. Yet they can also put people out of work or force people to do tasks in ways that seem regimented, unsuited to the pace and posture of human life. That comes about not just because machines are in the workplace, but because people can so easily be reduced to the status of "things." Henry Ford, founder of the Ford Motor Company and a pioneer in the use of the assembly line, is reputed to have said, "Why is it every time I ask for a pair of hands, they come with a brain attached?"[1]

Ford, like many early industrialists, was deeply influenced by the work of Frederick Winslow Taylor. A mechanical engineer by training, Taylor pioneered the field of systems engineering, figuring

---

1. Although this quote is widely attributed to Henry Ford, there is no definitive source.

out how to make repetitive physical labor more efficient by treating human beings as parts within a complex system of machinery. If the system is more efficient, Taylor reasoned, then business will be more profitable, resulting in better earnings for investors and higher wages for employees.[2]

Taylor was a controversial figure. He did much to advance the efficiency of workplaces, especially factories, in the early twentieth century, not only through his own studies and innovations but also by inspiring others to take up his cause. However, his critics charged him with creating efficiency at the cost of reducing people to automatons, depriving them of their innate human dignity. The dark side of Taylor's influence on factory work was famously satirized by Charlie Chaplin in the movie *Modern Times*. Chaplin's character goes to

Modern Times © Roy Export S.A.S. Scan Courtesy Cineteca di Bologna

In *Modern Times*, Charlie Chaplin plays a factory worker who becomes a cog in the industrial machine.

---

2. Frederick Winslow Taylor, *Principles of Scientific Management* (New York: Harper & Brothers, 1911).

work in a modern factory and, after a series of minor misadventures, gets transported on a conveyor belt into the bowels of the machinery. By the time he is rescued, he has been transformed. He dances around the factory floor applying his wrenches to everything he sees. The movie serves as a powerful comic warning about the potential of factory work to distort workers' sensibilities unless attention is paid to human needs.

As Taylor's ideas gained currency, more and more industries tried to find ways to implement his method of scientific management. A particularly famous example of this is the Hawthorne Studies. In 1927, Clarence Stoll and George Pennock initiated a research program at the Hawthorne Works plant of the Western Electric Company near Chicago. Their aim was to see how changes in working conditions would affect productivity.

The initial experiment studied the effects produced by increasing the lighting at workstations. They discovered that productivity went up. When light levels were increased again, productivity went up even more. But then something strange happened. When light levels were returned to former levels, productivity continued to climb.

The researchers were stumped. How could changes to working conditions have the same result even when the changes were reversed? Over the next several years, Western Electric expanded the experiments to see whether other changes would have similar effects on worker productivity.

The longest running study was conducted in a test room with stations where five young women assembled communications relays. The task was repetitive and monotonous. Each worker sat at a station, assembled a relay, and then dropped it into a hole. At the beginning of the experiment, the workers were averaging 2,400 relays per week. By the end of the first three months, making slight alterations to conditions at the stations, the workers were averaging 2,900 relays per week.[3] As more innovations were introduced, changes such as shorter working hours, rest breaks, and wage incentives also resulted in increased production.

---

3. See Michael Anteby and Rakesh Khurana, "The Human Relations Movement: Harvard Business School and the Hawthorne Experiments (1924–1933)," *http://www.library.hbs.edu/hc/hawthorne/*, and E.A.M. Gale, "The Hawthorne Studies: A Fable for Our Times?" *QJM* 97, no. 7 (2004): 439–49.

The findings continued to puzzle the Western Electric researchers until they brought in Harvard Business School professor Elton Mayo as a consultant. He suggested the workers were not responding to changed physical conditions so much as to the increased attention their work was receiving. The workers were being observed; they were being interviewed; the company was paying attention to their suggestions. They were beginning to find their work important, not just because of what they produced, but because of what they *thought* about what they produced. Mayo observed, "Opinions are not detachable. What a worker thinks on a certain subject cannot be torn out of their personal context and exhibited as significant."[4]

Observers noticed that the operators in the test room functioned as a team. They told stories, laughed, and joked with one another. Years later, one of the operators recalled, "We've been the best friends since the day we were in the test room."[5] The only time productivity declined markedly was in 1932 when, due to the economic conditions of the Great Depression, Western Electric was forced to cut 80 percent of its workforce. One might suppose that when the company notified the operators of their impending dismissal, productivity might have increased even more over the last few weeks as they took advantage of wage incentives to boost their income just before becoming unemployed. Instead, productivity dropped sharply. "We lost our pride," one of them observed years later.[6]

Human Nature

An essential aspect of human nature is rationality, the ability to think and act on the basis of reason. Physical objects, like rocks, chairs, bungee cords, or computers, can be acted upon, and they can even react, according to the natural laws governing them. If you drop a

---

4. Elton Mayo, *The Human Problems of an Industrial Civilization* (Cambridge, MA: Harvard University Press, 1933). Quoted in Gale, "Hawthorne Studies," 445.

5. Jeffrey A. Sonnenfeld, "Shedding Light on the Hawthorne Studies," *Journal of Occupational Behavior* 6 (1985): 124.

6. T.N. Whitehead, *The Industrial Worker: A Statistical Study of Human Relations in a Group of Manual Workers* (Cambridge, MA: Harvard University Press, 1938). Quoted in Gale, "Hawthorne Studies," 445.

rock from a tall building, it will strike the ground with predictable force, depending on factors like mass and wind. If you enter data into a computer, it will calculate results in accordance with whatever program it is running. Because human beings have a physical nature (bodies), it is possible to conduct experiments on them and see how they react to various stimuli, just as with any object. But because human beings also have a mental nature (minds), such studies always have an element of unpredictability. Human beings respond not only to the stimuli presented but also to what they think about the stimuli.

One way of thinking about this is to note that people are both objects and subjects. Their objective nature is explained by laws governing cause and effect and is studied by the traditional scientific disciplines such as biology, chemistry, and physics. Their subjective nature is explained by reasons and is studied by disciplines in the humanities, such as philosophy, theology, literature, and the fine arts. But, in actuality, the dividing line between objective and subjective nature is not so clearly defined.

Consider, for example, how one goes about explaining something as simple as turning off a light. Imagine two people at home in their living room one evening. Suddenly the light near Kathy's chair goes out. Kathy looks up from her book and asks Dave, "Why did the light go out?" Dave could give a number of responses:

1. "Sarah flipped the switch."
2. "I think Leah turned it off. They've been talking about conservation at school, and she's been going around the house all day looking for ways to save energy."
3. "Sorry. I must have turned it off when I walked out of the room. It's just a habit."

Dave's first answer refers to the physical causes of the light going out. Sarah's action is part of a chain of causes that has a predictable effect: When the switch is flipped, it interrupts the circuit supplying electrical current to the light bulb, and the bulb goes off. Although Kathy ostensibly asks a question about *why* the light went out, Dave's first answer refers to *how* it went out. (Our everyday language often fails to distinguish reasons from causes.) Dave's second answer refers to a reason. He implies that Leah turned the light out because she wanted to save energy. That was her purpose in flipping the switch. His third answer refers to a habitual action, an explanation that falls in between cause and reason. Dave didn't mean to turn out the light, so he can't give a purpose for doing it. He is also not referring to a simple chain of causes. He is referring to something less determinate, somewhere between *why* and *how*.

Much of what is studied in the social sciences, like psychology and sociology, resides in this region somewhere between reasons and causes, between peoples' subjective nature and their objective nature. The ways in which mental and physical aspects of human nature combine to produce behavior are complicated, and our efforts to understand the process are made even more complicated because the ways people think about things can be significantly influenced by conditions about which people are unaware.

For example, it is generally assumed that the domain of ethical responsibility is confined to intentional behavior. Kathy could hold Leah responsible for turning off the light because she meant to do it. But what about Sarah? Since Kathy does not have any information about Sarah's reason for flipping the switch, she does not know whether she did it intentionally or unintentionally, and if intentionally, whether her reason(s) might be justifiable. And in Dave's case, it seems he flipped the switch by accident, not for any particular reason. It was an automatic reaction, something he typically does when walking out of the room. However, he does have a reason for developing the habit in the first place: he doesn't want to waste electricity.

In organizational settings, so much human interaction falls into this gray zone between strictly intentional and strictly unintentional behavior that defining what falls under the purview of ethical responsibility can be difficult. Nevertheless, what is done to human beings is always subject to ethical evaluation, because even though objective and subjective nature can be distinguished, they cannot be separated in the person. Generally speaking, one can say that it is unethical to treat human beings simply as objects because even though they are made up of physical stuff, they also have subjectivity. That is, human beings experience what happens to them. They think and feel. They know what it is like to undergo something. They create and respond to reason. To treat them as if their subjectivity were irrelevant is to do violence to their nature.

Immanuel Kant, the eighteenth-century Prussian philosopher, has provided the most fully articulated explanation of what it means to treat someone ethically. In *Grounding for the Metaphysics of Morals*, he writes,

> Rational beings are called persons inasmuch as their nature already marks them out as ends in themselves, i.e., as something which is not to be used merely as a means and hence there is imposed thereby a limit on all arbitrary use of such beings, which are thus objects of respect. Persons are, therefore, not merely subjective ends, whose existence as an effect of our actions has a value for us; but such beings are objective ends, i.e., exist as ends in themselves. Such an end is one for which there can be substituted no other end to which such beings should serve merely as means. . . . The practical imperative therefore will be the following: Act in such a way that you treat humanity, whether in your own person or in the person of another, always at the same time as an end and never simply as a means.[7]

When Kant says people should always be treated as ends, he is arguing that any attempt to use people just to get something one wants without first getting their consent is ethically illegitimate. For that reason, any kind of coercion, deception, or manipulation is impermissible, because those are the chief ways people try to get others to do something against or despite their will.

But Kant goes further. It is also wrong, he says, to treat oneself only as a means to an end. This is a matter of having self-respect, not being willing to compromise one's rationality, but rather, seeking opportunities to enhance one's rational decision-making capacity.

Such a principle may seem fairly straightforward, but in practice it is quite challenging, in part because the connections between the physical and mental aspects of human nature are so complex.

For instance, anybody who has spent much time with toddlers knows that they can become cranky and difficult when they do not get enough sleep or food. Adults, however, can be similarly

---

7. Immanuel Kant, *Grounding for the Metaphysics of Morals*, trans. James W. Ellington, 3rd ed. (Indianapolis: Hackett, 1993), 36.

influenced by tiredness or hunger. Sometimes what one thinks is a thoughtful, rational response to a situation may instead—or also—be a causal response to physical conditions. A recent study on the effects of low blood sugar on spousal relationships highlights this phenomenon.[8] Over a period of twenty-one days, 107 spouses were given a voodoo doll and some pins. They were told to stick the pins into the voodoo doll when they were angry with their spouse. The lower the participants' blood glucose levels, the more pins they stuck into the voodoo doll. (This is why couples should not discuss potentially divisive topics—like money or politics—before dinner. After eating, when their glucose levels are higher, they are less likely to become angry with one another.) The key point to note is that at the moment when anger is felt, spouses can nearly always give cogent reasons for their anger: "He always gets this way when he's been drinking" or "She never tells me where she's been!" Is a spouse's anger in such a case a rational response to a perceived wrong, or an effect of low blood sugar, or some combination of both?

A study of Israeli judges found that when reviewing applications by prisoners for parole, the percentage of favorable reviews started out fairly high and then declined steadily until the judges took a midday break. After returning to the reviews after a meal and a brief rest, the rates of favorable reviews returned to the same percentage as the early morning and then declined once again throughout the afternoon.[9] Another study revealed that people who hold a pencil in their mouth sideways (forcing a smile) find cartoons funnier than those who hold a pencil in their mouth endwise (forcing a frown).[10]

Studies like these fall into an area of research known as "embodied cognition." The ways in which human beings think about themselves, others, and the world around them is profoundly influenced

---

8. Brad J. Bushman et al., "Low Glucose Relates to Greater Aggression in Married Couples," *Proceedings of the National Academy of Sciences* 111, no. 17 (2014): 6254–57.

9. Shai Danziger et al., "Extraneous Factors in Judicial Decisions," *Proceedings of the National Academy of Sciences* 108, no. 17 (2011): 6889–92. It could be that declining approval rates among the judges are not due to blood sugar levels so much as mental fatigue. See Maarten A.S. Boksema and Mattie Topsc, "Mental Fatigue: Costs and Benefits," *Brain Research Reviews* 59, no. 1 (2008): 125–39.

10. Daniel Kahneman, *Thinking Fast and Slow* (New York: Farrar, Straus and Giroux, 2011), 54.

by physical conditions like the surrounding environment, physical health, posture, facial expressions, bodily movements, and so on. The implications of such findings for the ethical responsibility of leaders in shaping workplace conditions are enormous. When one alters the physical conditions of the workplace to enhance productivity, is one manipulating workers or merely increasing their rational capacity? Perhaps it depends on precisely what is done and why.

It is one thing to use research in ergonomics to determine which office chairs are most likely to reduce back and shoulder strain and thereby lessen costs stemming from lost work days. But how can businesses legitimately make use of research showing that interactions with coworkers improve among those who use workstation treadmills?[11] Or what about recent efforts to track every detail of every employee's actions? Consider how companies are applying such human dynamics research today:

> Ben Waber is chief executive of Sociometric Solutions, a start-up that grew out of his doctoral research at M.I.T.'s Human Dynamics Laboratory, which conducts research in the new technologies. Sociometric Solutions advises companies using sensor-rich ID badges worn by employees. These sociometric badges, equipped with two microphones, a location sensor and an accelerometer, monitor the communications behavior of individuals—tone of voice, posture and body language, as well as who spoke to whom for how long.
>
> Sociometric Solutions is already working with twenty companies in the banking, technology, pharmaceutical and health care industries, involving thousands of employees. . . . The payoff for well-designed workplace monitoring . . . can be significant. The underlying theme of human dynamics research is that people are social learners, so arranging work to increase productive face-to-face communication yields measurable benefits.[12]

---

11. Avner Ben-Ner et al., "Treadmill Workstations: The Effects of Walking while Working on Physical Activity and Work Performance," *PLOS ONE* 9, no. 2 (2014): e88620.

12. Steve Lohr, "Unblinking Eyes Track Employees," *New York Times*, June 21, 2014, A1.

As technology gets more sophisticated, more and more reliable information is being produced about how to increase productivity by integrating human behavior seamlessly into a complex social/ technological system. During Taylor's age, efficiency improvements were limited to changing various physical conditions such as lighting or seating and seeing how people responded to those changes. The Hawthorne Studies revealed that more important even than physical conditions are the social conditions: how workers are treated, whether they are listened to by their supervisors, whether they are treated with respect, whether their roles are regarded as meaningful. In today's workplace, as new technological developments provide the opportunities for an increased focus on the gray zone between causes and reasons, between the physical and the mental world that makes up so much of human life, the ethical concerns raised by such developments are not just that humans may be replaced by machines, but rather that the very conditions of human interaction may be manipulated in ways that profoundly shape how people think and act without them even being aware of it.

Servant Leadership

In 1926, Robert K. Greenleaf was a senior at Carleton College in Northfield, Minnesota, taking a course by Dr. Oscar C. Helming on the sociology of labor problems. The course became a pivotal point in Greenleaf's life. Years later, he looked back on Helming's influence:

> One day, in the course of a rambling lecture, he made a statement like this: "We are becoming a nation of large institutions. . . . Everything is getting big—government, churches, businesses, labor unions, universities—and none of these big institutions are [sic] serving well, either the people whom they are set up to serve or the people who staff them to render the service. Now, you can do as I do: stand outside and suggest, encourage, try to bring pressure on them to do better. But nothing happens, nothing changes, until somebody who is established inside with his hands on the levers of power and influence, and who knows how to change things, decides to respond. These institutions can

be bludgeoned, coerced, threatened from the outside. But they can only be changed from the inside by somebody who knows how to do it *and who wants to do it.* Some of you folks ought to make your careers inside these institutions and become the ones who respond to the idea that they could do better."[13]

That is just what Greenleaf did. He got a job working on a line crew installing and repairing telephone lines with Ohio Bell, a subsidiary of AT&T, which at the time was the world's largest company, with nearly half a million employees. He quickly moved up, benefitting from AT&T's early experiments in management training, eventually getting invited to join the staff of the operations and engineering department at the company's headquarters in New York. The new position allowed him to travel across the country to the various divisions of AT&T. His role was to investigate and solve seemingly intractable organizational problems, and it gave him the opportunity to observe firsthand how large organizations function. It also gave him the opportunity to meet, and learn from, the principal investigators of the Hawthorne Studies at Western Electric.[14]

Even as the research at Hawthorne was winding down, Greenleaf was taking its lessons and applying them to leadership training programs at AT&T. He developed a formal listening course in 1939. And he began formulating the ideas that would be expressed three decades later in his revolutionary work, *The Servant as Leader.*[15]

In that essay, he articulated a vision that continues to inspire people today: the best leaders are those who have a deep personal commitment to the common good—that is, to the well-being of all and not just a few select individuals, and out of that commitment comes the desire to lead. What this means is that leadership cannot be defined in terms of principles, or techniques, or strategies; it is primarily a matter of attitude, originating in love and culminating in effective action. Of course, there is much more to it than that.

---

13. Don M. Frick, *Robert K. Greenleaf: A Life of Servant Leadership* (San Francisco: Berrett-Koehler, 2004), 76.

14. Ibid., 167.

15. Robert K. Greenleaf, *The Servant as Leader* (Westfield, IN: Greenleaf Center for Servant Leadership, 2008).

The foundational insight of servant leadership is the notion that people's best selves are motivated by altruism, a sincere interest in the well-being of others. If leaders want people to follow them willingly, and if they want people to bring their whole selves, fully engaged, into the workplace, then they must practice persuasion rather than manipulation or coercion.

The dominant conception of leadership in US society is the ability to effectively wield power or authority to achieve some goal—no matter what that goal happens to be. Most leadership books focus on techniques that enable one to "get ahead" in the race with competing individuals and organizations.

Greenleaf didn't see things that way. He thought of leadership as an obligation to improve people's lives through effective service. Leadership does not consist of techniques or strategies to achieve some arbitrary goal. It should, instead, focus on the achievement of the common good. Any methods employed by a leader proceed from the commitment to that end. Leadership, in other words, is not a value-neutral subject; rather, it is an exercise of virtue, something that can be evaluated according to whether it leads to a flourishing life for individuals and communities.[16]

When Greenleaf retired from his thirty-eight-year career with AT&T, he founded the Center for Applied Ethics in order to help leaders in organizations become more ethical and effective. Recalling Helming's lecture from years before, and recognizing that institutions had indeed become more and more influential in society, he urged that the way to make society better was to work through institutions.

> This is my thesis: caring for persons, the more able and the less able serving each other, is the rock upon which a good society is built. Whereas, until recently, caring was largely person to person, now most of it is mediated through institutions—often large, complex, powerful, impersonal; not always competent; sometimes corrupt. If a better society is to be built, one that is more just and more loving, one that provides greater creative opportunity for its people, then the most open course is to raise both the capacity to serve and the very performance

---

16. For ancient Greek philosophers, particularly Aristotle, the whole point of ethics was to lead a life of *eudaimonia*, usually translated as "flourishing" or "happiness."

as servant of existing major institutions by new regenerative forces operating within them.[17]

A fairly common criticism of this notion of leadership is that it is "soft," "weak," or "not realistic." But Greenleaf argued that it is in fact more realistic than the more hierarchical, power-based forms of leadership that critics tend to favor, because it is based on a positive conception of human nature. It leverages the power of altruism to motivate. For that reason, servant leadership leads to stronger, healthier, more resilient organizations. As far as being "soft" or "weak," such criticisms are based on a misconception that because servant leadership discourages the use of coercive power, it inevitably results in a permissive culture in which "anything goes." Instead, servant leadership requires more strength, discipline, and persistence than power-based leadership because it commits one to leading through persuasion. Such a commitment takes time; it requires foresight and planning. It also requires much more attention to the ways in which people interact with one another. It is more demanding on the leader's part because it requires a well-developed imagination and a robust understanding of how seemingly isolated events fit into the big picture.

Coercive power is frequently employed by people who lack the imagination to see any other means of achieving their goals. For such people, power tends to become the tool of first choice rather than the last resort. A type of leadership that does not choose power first can easily seem incomprehensible to those who know no other way.

Thomas Jefferson found himself in that situation repeatedly, first as the governor of Virginia and later as the third president of the United States. In Garry Wills' book, *Inventing America*, Wills points out that Jefferson not only sought to limit the power of the government through the Bill of Rights, he also refrained from exercising the power that was available to him, and indeed expected of him, as an executive: "He exasperated others by seeing inevitability where they saw only crisis, by a long-range vision that treated day-to-day struggles as already settled in their outcome."[18]

---

17. Robert K. Greenleaf, "The Institution as Servant," in *Servant Leadership: A Journey into the Nature of Legitimate Power and Greatness* (New York: Paulist Press, 1977), 49.

18. Garry Wills, *Inventing America: Jefferson's Declaration of Independence* (New York: Doubleday, 1978), 30.

An example of Jefferson's restraint is demonstrated by a letter he wrote to James Madison on January 30, 1787, urging him not to use armed force to put down a rebellion:

> I am impatient to learn your sentiments on the late troubles in the Eastern States. So far as I have yet seen, they do not appear to threaten serious consequences. Those states have suffered by the stoppage of the channels of their commerce, which have not yet found other issue. This must render money scarce and make the people uneasy. This uneasiness has produced acts absolutely unjustifiable; but I hope they will produce no severities from their governments. A consciousness of those in power that their administration of public affairs has been honest may perhaps produce too great a degree of indignation; and those characters wherein fear predominates over hope may apprehend too much from these instances of irregularity. They may conclude too hastily that nature has formed man insusceptible of any other government than that of force, a conclusion which is not founded in truth, nor experience.[19]

Jefferson's letter to Madison illustrates why leadership cannot be reduced to a selection of "techniques" or "strategies." Techniques and strategies are merely means to an end, and if one does not understand how a situation is unfolding, what motivations are driving the people involved, and how the events are likely to turn out, one is unlikely to be able to identify what means should be employed or how they should be employed. Jefferson refers specifically to the virtue of hope, which allows one to see things whole, in contrast to fear, which tends to constrict one's vision. One should note also that Jefferson refers to hope, not optimism. They are similar concepts, but the distinction is significant. As the philosopher Newton Garver points out, "Hope is the confidence that things can work out somehow or other, and optimism the confidence that things will work out as planned."[20] As

---

19. Thomas Jefferson, "Letter to James Madison," in *Jefferson: Writings*, ed. Merrill D. Peterson (New York: Library of America, 1984), 881–82.

20. Newton Garver, *Jesus, Jefferson, and the Task of Friends* (Wallingford, PA: Pendle Hill, 1983), 14. I am indebted to Garver's essay for this entire discussion of Jefferson on power and restraint.

such, optimism tends to take the form of confidence in specific plans or strategies whereas hope tends to take the form of confidence in people, fate, or divine providence. Hope is a fundamental trust that the goodness inherent in human nature will prevail in the long run.

Jefferson's letter to Madison illustrates his conviction that leadership requires virtue, because virtue shapes perception. Without virtue, even the best techniques and strategies will be employed in the wrong ways, or at the wrong times, or on the wrong people.

To take just one example, consider the simple technique of listening. Abundant literature points to the importance of listening to employees in order to keep them engaged, to learn important insights about the organization, and, in brief, to keep an organization operating effectively. And yet, many leaders fail to listen thoroughly and intentionally. Greenleaf observes, "Only a true natural servant automatically responds to any problem by listening *first*."[21] In other words, the inclination to listen first must be rooted in one's character in order to be done habitually. If not, a person will fall back into old patterns of behavior under conditions of hurry or stress, often when attentive listening is most needed.

Organizational Heroes
TOM GREEN AND MARY MILLER

In 2006, Tom Green and Mary Miller found themselves in a demanding situation. Tom was the plant manager and Mary the human resources director for the Delphi Automotive brake assembly operation in Dayton, Ohio, a facility that employed 1,600 people. They were charged with overseeing a two-year shutdown of the plant after Delphi declared bankruptcy. But there was a catch. Because Delphi supplied brake components to General Motors, they had to continue producing one million high-quality parts per month until new suppliers were able to take over, a process

Continued

---

21. Greenleaf, *The Servant as Leader*, 18.

that would not be completed until 2008. How could a manufacturing plant continue operating at full capacity after a shutdown had been announced while also maintaining exacting standards of quality control? Within a few months of the announcement, 40 percent of the salaried workforce and 84 percent of the hourly workers had resigned. New workers, knowing that they had no long-term future with the company, had to be hired and trained.

The only guidance Tom and Mary had came from Delphi's long-standing four corporate goals: safety, quality, delivery, and cost. But they knew that they needed something more, something that would engage a temporary workforce and keep them focused. So they adopted four principles of Servant Leadership:

- Listen, don't talk.
- Ask employees, "What do you need?"
- Set aside time every week for foresight and planning.
- Ask, "Do those served grow as persons?"

Using these four principles, Tom and Mary had the managers go throughout the plant, sit down to talk individually with employees, and develop a plan of action only after they had gathered input from everyone. The managers listened to the fears expressed by many of the employees and committed themselves to complete honesty and transparency. Every Friday, Tom and Mary set aside time for a two-hour strategy session. No matter what crisis came up, that two-hour time was used not for responding to immediate needs but for preparing for the future. They established robust training programs, helping employees prepare for new careers by developing résumé writing, interviewing, and networking skills. Every employee had a minimum of forty hours of career training. One individual remarked at the end of the process,

> After twenty-nine years at GM/Delphi, I did so many new things during the last two years that I was able to

Continued

> **Organizational Heroes:** TOM GREEN AND MARY MILLER *Continued*
>
> see that I could adapt and learn to do something completely outside my experience and comfort zone.[22]
>
> The career training program was so successful, so valued by employees, that it actually extended the time they stayed on at Delphi. The employees were learning so much they did not want to leave until they had to do so.
>
> More than anything else, Tom and Mary worked and succeeded at building a culture of trust. They listened, they responded, and their employees responded as well. Not only did Tom and Mary succeed in keeping the plant operating, in every key measurement—safety, quality, delivery, and cost—but also the brake assembly operations improved.
>
>> In the face of seemingly insurmountable obstacles, we had become one of the safest manufacturing operations in America, our defect rate was single digit parts per million, our on-time delivery was 99.5 percent, and our financial performance was the best it had been in decades. On that last day, we were the best we had ever been.[23]
>
> Tom and Mary's only regret was knowing that if the plant had operated with a commitment to trust, honesty, and openness from the beginning, there would have been no need to close it down.

Servant leadership is not simply a method, style, or technique; it is a philosophy of leadership based in a commitment to the common good and oriented by an attitude of service. That is why Greenleaf never tried to reduce servant leadership to a simple set of principles. The closest he came to a brief description was this:

---

22. Tom Green and Mary Miller, *Servant Leadership in Hard Times: The Closing of the Delphi Brake Assembly Operations* (Westfield, IN: Greenleaf Center for Servant Leadership, 2012), 21.

23. Ibid, 9.

The best test, and difficult to administer, is, do those served grow as persons? Do they, while being served, become healthier, wiser, freer, more autonomous, more likely themselves to become servants? And, what is the effect on the least privileged in society? Will they benefit or at least not be further deprived?[24]

Greenleaf did not invent servant leadership; he merely wrote about ideas he picked up from paying attention to others, ideas that he then found confirmed by his own experience at AT&T. One of those others whom Greenleaf credits was Herman Hesse, whose novel *The Journey to the East* ends with the main character relating a conversation with his mentor, Leo: "We had talked about the creations of poetry being more vivid and real than the poets themselves."[25] This sentence is a beautiful expression of the effect of the servant leader on the follower, whether that leader is a business owner, a corporate supervisor, a trustee, a politician, a pastor, a parent, or a teacher. He or she draws attention so effectively to the goodness of the work—its purpose or significance—that the followers may forget who directed their attention to it in the first place.

The Importance of Purpose

Leaders of organizations who neglect to emphasize the purpose of their organization's work, that is, its mission, fail to capitalize on the most powerful motivating influence available to human beings. Having a shared purpose that is genuinely meaningful can bring people together, inspire them, and cause them to want to do good work.

Viktor Frankl, the Jewish concentration camp survivor and psychiatrist who wrote *Man's Search for Meaning*, quoted Nietzsche to explain what he observed at Auschwitz: "He who has a *why* to live, can bear with almost any *how*."[26] Frankl noticed that when people

---

24. Greenleaf, *The Servant as Leader*, 15.

25. Herman Hesse, *The Journey to the East*, trans. Hilda Rosner (New York: Picador, 1956), 118. Greenleaf writes about Hesse's influence on the development of his thought in *The Servant as Leader*.

26. Viktor E. Frankl, *Man's Search for Meaning: An Introduction to Logotherapy* (Boston: Beacon Press, 1959), 84.

lost hope, when they began to think there was no meaning in their suffering, they lost the ability to survive the harsh conditions of the camps. "Woe to him who saw no more sense in his life, no aim, no purpose, and therefore no point in carrying on. He was soon lost."[27]

The human need for purpose is neither trivial nor accidental. It is based in human nature, specifically in the fact that human beings consist of mind, body, and spirit. Mind is the function of reason, that part of the person that operates according to some goal or *telos*.[28] Mind is the part of a person that responds to *why*.

Organizations that fail to articulate a shared and compelling purpose are operating with less than full efficiency, like a six-cylinder car running on only four cylinders. They may still manage to get by, because humans are wonderfully adept at supplying their own purposes to activities. Ask several individuals employed by a company why they work there and you may get several different answers: "I'm providing for my family," "I've got some good friends who work here," "I'm just putting in time until retirement." Such answers are not bad reasons, nor even insubstantial. But they are not shared reasons; they bear no witness to a common good, and so they do not provide a means of resolving conflicts when struggles or difficulties arise.

Organizational Heroes
CHERYL AND RALPH BROETJE

Cheryl and Ralph met each other in traffic court. He was ticketed for driving too slowly—in a red Corvette; her ticket was for speeding—in a Ford station wagon. A year later, they were married and starting out on an adventure together that would change thousands of lives around the world.

Continued

---

27. Ibid., 85.

28. *Telos* is an ancient Greek word meaning "goal" or "purpose." From it we get the word "teleology," which means understanding the function of something by reference to its purpose. In ethics, an action is considered good in a teleological sense if it has a good purpose.

Organizational Heroes: CHERYL AND RALPH BROETJE *Continued*

Although they had no money, they had friends and a purpose. Their friends helped them secure a loan to purchase a small apple orchard. Their purpose was to use their earnings to help others. Since the time he was in junior high school, Ralph nurtured a dream of using the proceeds from an apple orchard to feed starving children in India. Years later, when he and Cheryl acquired their first orchard, they fulfilled that dream. It was that dream—a compelling vision of a higher purpose for their work—that sustained and guided them through their early struggles.

Today Broetje Orchards, selling apples and cherries under the "First Fruits of Washington" label, is one of the largest privately owned orchards in the world. It employs more than 1,100 people on a year-round basis and donates 75 percent of its profits to humanitarian causes around the world.

The Broetje's understood that the success of their business depended on the well-being of the people who worked for them, mostly seasonal workers traveling north to Washington from Mexico. If they wanted to stabilize their business, they needed to help their employees flourish, and that meant several things: finding ways to distribute the working opportunities year-round; building quality and affordable housing; building schools and churches; providing health care, day care, and early childhood education, and providing college scholarships for first-generation students. The depth and breadth of the Broetje's commitment is remarkable.

One story in particular demonstrates the way the Broetje's think about their orchard and its people. In 1992, they had to decide what to do about a fifty-acre plot of cherry trees that had failed to produce for four straight years. Would they convert it to apples or give it one more chance? For the Broetje's, such decisions are not merely financial, they are decisions about how to live, which, for them, involve moral and religious beliefs, considerations that provided much of their motivation for going into the orchard business in the first place. So Ralph and Cheryl prayed about the decision together, and they came across a parable about a man who planted

Continued

Organizational Heroes: CHERYL AND RALPH BROETJE *Continued*

a fig tree that had not produced fruit for several years. In the story, the man's gardener convinces him to give it one more year.[29]

They decided that, like the man in the parable, they could give their cherry trees one more year. If they did not yield fruit, the trees would be cut down and the land used for apples. If they did yield fruit, the Broetje's would donate all the proceeds to charity.

The following year, the cherry trees flourished, and Ralph and Cheryl kept their pledge, donating all of the proceeds to a children's home in Oaxaca, Mexico. But the Broetje's went even further. If they were serious about wanting to empower their employees, they thought the employees themselves should decide where the cherry profits should go. So they asked their workers to select a committee to represent them and gave that committee full authority to determine how the funds are spent. In 2013 the committee donated a total of $286,000 to fifteen charities in six countries, to organizations such as Medical Teams International in Guatemala and International Justice Mission in India. The year before they donated $400,000 to World Vision to help African children affected by HIV/AIDS.[30]

People are amazed when they first hear the story of the cherry orchard, but for the Broetje's, it was not a difficult decision. It flowed naturally from a shared understanding of their purpose in business, an understanding that is shared not just with each other but with their employees as well. Cheryl explains it this way:

> There's a relationship. We care for the land. The land cares for us. And we care for each other. There is love in the organization. It is about caring. People are the fruit that will last, so our orchards must bear fruit so we can bear fruit that will last.[31]

---

29. Luke 13:6–9.

30. Kari Costanza, "Birth of the Cherry Donations," *http://www.firstfruits.com /cherry-crop-donations.html*.

31. Jerry Glashagel, *Servant Institutions in Business* (Westfield, IN: Greenleaf Center for Servant Leadership, 2009), 18.

An ethical organization is characterized by successful integration of the three aspects of the person, with mind (*why*) leading body (*what*) and spirit (*how*). The *why* consists of the organization's mission, its goal or purpose. And it cannot be just any goal, but rather something that provides meaning for all those who have a stake in the organization because it connects them in relation to a common good. The *what* consists of the organization's resources: its people, buildings, financial assets, products, proprietary information, and so on. The *how* consists of the organization's power: its energy and drive. Whatever the organization does either intentionally or unintentionally to direct the way things get done—employing management strategies, implementing policies and procedures, providing bonuses or other incentives, fostering communication among employees—is an exercise of power.

Mission-led Organization

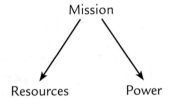

In a mission-led organization, a focus on purpose (mission) determines what is needed (resources) and how things should be done (power).

In the illustration, note that mission is at the top. It is the leader's responsibility to direct attention toward the mission first, so that all decisions regarding power and resources are made in light of the organization's shared purpose. If the leader neglects to do that, the organization will flip one way or the other, with either resources or power becoming the focus of the organization, and the shared purpose or meaning of the organization will be abandoned or overshadowed.

How this plays out in day-to-day situations can be illustrated by considering a number of different scenarios.

Scenario One: Focus on Resources

Roger has a problem. Three different employees have come to him in the last few weeks with complaints about Bob, his top salesperson.

They claim Bob is verbally abusive, ridiculing and demeaning other employees in the company. When Roger looks into the allegations, he finds no evidence Bob has violated federal harassment laws, but there is no question that he violated company policies requiring employees to treat one another with respect. In fact, Bob obviously went out of his way to make life miserable for several people in the company. The worst thing is that Bob denies any wrongdoing. "What's the big deal?" he replies when Roger questions him. "If some people can't take a little joke now and then, that's their problem." Roger doesn't know whether the company can continue to perform at its current levels without Bob, and he is worried about losing Bob's clients. He wonders whether the employees who complained to him would be satisfied if he makes Bob take an ethics course.

Analysis

Roger is afraid of dealing with this situation directly and honestly. He is letting concern about resources take priority in his decision making. His solution of making Bob take an ethics course is not really intended to change Bob's behavior; rather, Roger is hoping that the "punishment" will be enough to silence the complainers. The likely result is that Bob will have even more power in the company—a greater ability to assert his dominance and negatively affect other employees' morale. Roger needs to remind himself of the company's mission and of his primary responsibility to all the employees.

Resource-led Organization

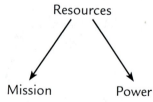

In a resources-led organization, a focus on what is needed (resources) determines how things are done (power) and why they should be done (mission).

Scenario Two: Focus on Power

Julie is the human resources director at a large company that is undergoing major restructuring. Executives in the company are worried about employee engagement, and their worries are well-founded. Over the next several months, some employees will be laid off, some will be given the option to relocate, and many will find that they have new responsibilities and different supervisors. Julie has been asked to make sure that morale stays high during this stressful transition.

She recalls attending a leadership conference a couple of years earlier with the theme of managing change. One of the keynote speakers at the conference, William U. Duet, was especially memorable. He was super positive and upbeat. At the end of his talk, everyone gave him a standing ovation. Julie decides to contact Will to see whether he can come to her company and give his motivational speech, "From Surviving to Thriving: Six Steps to 110 Percent." But Julie wants to make sure the message really takes hold, so she also orders copies of *Who Moved My Cheese?*, a popular parable about dealing with change, for every employee.[32]

Analysis

Julie is focused exclusively on engaging the spirit of employees in the company. To be fair, that is all she was asked to do, but if she does not find a way to link her strategies for dealing with change

Power-led Organization

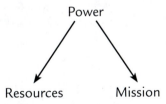

In a power-led organization, a focus on how things are done (power) determines what is needed (resources) and why things should be done (mission).

---

32. Spencer Johnson, *Who Moved My Cheese? An Amazing Way to Deal with Change in Your Work and in Your Life* (New York: G.P. Putnam's Sons, 1998).

to the overall mission of the company, the impact will be superficial. At best, her efforts will result in a short-term "bump" in morale. At worst, she may alienate a certain portion of the employees who resent being manipulated and also silence the employees who care most about the company, by creating the perception that legitimate questions about restructuring are evidence of a negative attitude and an inability to accept change.

Scenario Three: Lack of Focus

Jared is really pumped up. Beth, the executive director of Better Lives for Children, Inc., has asked him to be part of a team to draft a new strategic plan. Even though he has only worked for the nonprofit a few months, he is excited about sharing his ideas for improvement. He believes wholeheartedly in the good work they do on behalf of children in the city, but he also sees ways they can improve.

The planning team holds several sessions, getting valuable input from board members, donors, clients, and representatives of local government. There are some struggles along the way, but the team is committed and they succeed in writing up a compelling new mission and vision statement along with a set of clearly defined and practical goals. Jared can't wait to see the plan put into action.

Weeks go by and then months, but Jared doesn't see any significant changes in the organization. One day Jared shares his disappointment with Jim, a colleague who has worked there for nearly two decades. "Oh, you shouldn't be surprised," Jim says. "We go through strategic planning every few years, but nothing ever comes of it. Everybody knows our mission is to help children. That's all that matters."

Analysis

Jared is discovering that he works for an organization with a mission that is disengaged from its operations. Everybody he talks to seems to believe in the mission. That's not the problem. It's just that no practical decisions about budgeting or communications or anything else seem to follow from it. Maybe they did at one time, when the organization was founded, but it seems like most of the daily operations function on autopilot now.

Disconnected Organization

In a disconnected organization, discussions of purpose (mission) do not practically influence what is needed (resources) or how things are done (power).

Scenario Four: Focus on Mission

Tiffany gets up early Friday morning. She wants to make sure she has some quiet time to think about her team's weekly meeting before the hustle and bustle of the day. She goes over the key parts of the agenda in her mind: "Let's see . . . Tim is going to open with a reflection. That's good. He always prepares something thoughtful and inspiring. It will remind everyone why we are here and set a good example for the new team members. Then we need to discuss changes to the sick leave policy. Maybe I should start by asking Sarah what she thinks first. She's so quiet, her voice could get drowned out once we really get into the discussion, but her opinion carries more weight than she realizes. I'll make a note to remind myself. The big issue today is going to be the recent drop in sales. I don't want to worry the team too much, but it could mean big changes if we don't turn things around. I've got a few ideas, but I'd like to see what they suggest first."

She looks up from her desk and sees a quote from Robert Greenleaf that she discovered recently and put on the wall:

> Whereas the usual assumption about the firm is that it is in business to make a profit and serve its customers and that it does things for and to employees to get them to be productive, the new ethic requires that growth of those who do the work is the primary aim, and the workers then see to it that the customer is served and that the ink on the bottom line is black.[33]

---

33. Greenleaf, *Servant Leadership*, 145.

Analysis

Tiffany starts every meeting with some kind of reflection, rotating the responsibility among the different members of the team. Regardless of how pressed they are for time, she never neglects the reflection. She understands that whatever you start with, you get more of. If she wants the team's attention to be focused on their common purpose, she needs to start each meeting by giving everyone an opportunity to reorient so that when they begin discussing potentially controversial issues they don't simply react out of fear or self-interest. She also thinks about how to elicit the contribution of everyone on the team by reminding herself to listen first. She is taking care to make sure that the energy of the team proceeds from their active participation in decision making. She saves the issue of declining sales, which will most likely lead to discussions about the budget, to the end of the meeting, after they have already spent time focusing together on their common purpose. Finally, she understands that leading other people is a tremendous responsibility. She keeps herself refreshed and focused by reading and learning, finding new ways to put good ideas into practice.

Conclusion

As society continues to advance in technology and in the scientific understanding of systems and processes, increasingly sophisticated ways of manipulating people become available, more ways of exploiting the gray zone between their objective and subjective natures. To counter this trend, society requires leaders within organizations who care about people, who are inclined to listen first, who know how to treat people as ends, who understand that people inevitably bring their best selves forward when one appeals to the good within them.

Remember Taylor, whose work influenced industrialists like Henry Ford? He believed that by making companies more profitable, the wages of employees could be increased, thus providing a benefit to everyone: workers, managers, and shareholders. But his methods were frequently used to boost earnings for shareholders with little or no benefit going to the workers. The ethical problem was that Taylor's approach treated workers solely as means, as objects to be used to increase profits. And that is unethical even if the profits are shared with employees for their own benefit. An ethical approach necessarily treats the employees themselves as ends, not just as means to an end.

An ethical organization is one that has a virtuous culture, is characterized by wisdom, temperance, and courage, and is comprised of people who know how to lead by persuasion and inspiration.

Discussion Questions

1. What did the Hawthorne studies reveal about efficiency in the workplace?

2. Immanuel Kant claimed that you should always treat people as ends in themselves and never as means to an end. What are some examples of treating people as means or as ends?

3. What are some of the most significant ethical concerns raised by the increasing use of technology in the workplace?

4. Do you know anyone who might be described as a "servant leader"? What virtues do you see in that person?

Resources for Further Exploration

Print

Frick, Don M. *Robert K. Greenleaf: A Life of Servant Leadership*. San Francisco: Berrett-Koehler, 2004.

> Frick's biography of Greenleaf is an especially valuable resource for anyone interested in the history of servant leadership and its relation to other leadership theories.

Greenleaf, Robert K. *The Servant as Leader*. Westfield, IN: Greenleaf Center for Servant Leadership, 2008.

> This pamphlet is the best introduction to Greenleaf's work.
>
> Numerous other books by and about Greenleaf can be found on the website of the Greenleaf Center for Servant Leadership (*https://www.greenleaf.org/*).

OTHER MEDIA

"The Year They Discovered People." 2011. *http://techchannel.att
.com/play-video.cfm/2011/11/28/AT&T-Archives-The-Year
-They-Discovered-People.* Time: 00:15:39.

This documentary film from the AT&T archives contains interviews with some of the people involved in the original Hawthorne Studies.

CHAPTER 3

Power, Trust, and Meaning

On the morning of November 3, 2014, Gary Anderson was delivering a load of drywall to a construction site in Jersey City. A worker installing windows on the fiftieth floor of the building accidentally dropped his tape measure. It fell five hundred feet, reaching an estimated speed of 140 mph, bounced off a piece of metal, and hit Anderson in the head, killing him. Because he was only going to be there a few minutes, he had left his hard hat on the backseat of his car.[1]

Anyone entering a construction site like the one in Jersey City is required to wear a hard hat, not because accidents precisely like the one that befell Mr. Anderson are commonplace but because so many different kinds of serious accidents can happen. Accidents, even those that are unpredictable, are often preventable.

Many workplaces have rules in place to ensure physical safety—requirements for things like hard hats, steel-toe shoes, respirator masks, harnesses, and so on. The rules are necessitated by the very conditions that make certain places and certain types of work potentially dangerous. They provide common standards for everyone, regardless of differences in perception, experience, or understanding of the conditions that give rise to them. Yet the people who make and enforce those rules need to know why they are important even when they might seem inconvenient or unnecessary. Such knowledge requires a general understanding that goes beyond the particularities of the rules themselves, an understanding of conditions such as gravity, velocity, force, electricity, heat, cold, toxins, and so on.

---

1. Dana Sauchelli, Leonica Valentine, and Danika Fears, "Tape Measure Falls 50 Stories, Killing Worker," *New York Post*, November 3, 2014.

In a similar way, workplaces have rules to protect employees from the actions of other employees—policies regarding behaviors like sexual harassment, emotional and physical abuse, and discrimination. Just as with rules for physical safety, such policies are necessitated by the conditions that give rise to them—the conditions of human nature.

Every well-intentioned rule is established to secure some good purpose, such as personal safety, a healthy environment, fair competition, and improved achievement. Rules are informed by people's experience of past events, but they are also limited by the rule makers' predictive imagination about what is likely to happen in the future. Occasionally, situations arise when enforcement of a rule conflicts with the very purpose the rule is intended to protect,[2] and in such cases it may be prudent or even necessary to make an exception. This is the function of practical wisdom, determining which means are appropriate to the desired ends.

Aristotle considered practical wisdom (*phronēsis*) to be the most important of the virtues. It is the ability to judge when an action is appropriate or inappropriate by considering the relevant factors, such as time, place, motivation, intent, and outcome. In order to adequately take such factors into account, one must have knowledge of the conditions at play in the context of the rules.

Organizational Hero
CHUCK DRISCOLL

When Chuck Driscoll was hired by Marshalls in 1970, the Boston-based discount clothing retailer had only three stores. As a young man fresh out of college, Chuck did not have any management experience and, working in a company that was still trying

Continued

---

2. Consider, for example, a well-intentioned but poorly crafted gift policy that is intended to protect a firm's reputation but ends up offending potential clients, or a policy that restricts employee socializing in order to prevent interpersonal conflicts but which results in decreased employee engagement. An instance of the former type of case will be discussed in chapter 5; the latter type of case is discussed later in this chapter.

Organizational Hero: CHUCK DRISCOLL *Continued*

to define its own culture, he did not receive much guidance. He had to find his own answer to the question, what does it mean to be a good manager?

Chuck quickly realized he needed two things: more experience in retail and better people skills. So he left Marshalls to assume a position as a merchandise buyer for another company and then took time out to earn a master's degree in counseling. When he returned to Marshalls four years later, Chuck had more confidence and a clearer vision of how to lead others. He understood that success as a store manager depended on getting results from other people, and he understood that the success of Marshalls as a whole depended on maximizing performance at every level. As a result, he began developing the people under his charge.

Chuck was promoted quickly from store manager to district manager, then to regional manager in Chicago, and finally to vice president of administration for Marshalls' Store Operations at their corporate headquarters in Boston. During that time Marshalls grew from approximately $10 million in annual sales to more than $2 billion. That kind of growth required the organization to define itself, and Chuck was a major factor in the development of Marshalls' culture.

Much of Chuck's career was focused on creating successful training programs for managers. He focused on internal recruitment and retention so successfully that while the other regions were spending millions of dollars every year on recruitment fees, Chuck's region spent nothing at all. As he put it, "If you have good human resources programming, it optimizes your ability to achieve profits for the company." But that meant more than just starting a new program; it meant standing up for people at crucial times. One occasion when Chuck had to do that was in 1985 when he promoted Donna Price.

Donna was a bright, charismatic store manager in Minneapolis. A natural leader, other people in the district looked up to her. When a vacancy opened up in the district manager position,

Continued

Organizational Hero: CHUCK DRISCOLL *Continued*

she was the obvious choice. Except for one thing: Donna was the wrong sex.

When Chuck called his boss, the vice president of store operations, to inform him of his decision, the conversation went something like this:

VP: "Chuck, do you like working for Marshalls?"

Chuck: "Is that a threat?"

VP: "You can take it however you like. But there's never been a woman district manager at Marshalls, and there won't be any time soon."

Chuck did not accept defeat. He immediately removed all identifying characteristics from the résumés of the job candidates and flew to Boston. He placed the stack of résumés on the VP's desk. "You choose the best one," he said.

The VP chose Donna's résumé.

"I'm glad you agree with me," said Chuck. He flew back to Chicago and promoted Donna.

One of Chuck's greatest strengths is his creativity in finding solutions to ethical problems where others see only obstacles. "In my experience," he said, "I rarely ran into an individual who did not want to do a good job. But I often found that the organization would stand in the way of getting the results they wanted, by not providing the resources and support people need to do their job well." He continued, "I looked at my whole career as an exercise in ethics. But that is not necessarily congruent with corporate processes."

When the process gets in the way of doing the right thing, Chuck changes the process.

No matter what kind of business one is in, whether for-profit or not-for-profit, no matter what kind of role one has, whether owner or employee, supervisor or supervised, paid staff member or volunteer, most ethical issues arise out of problems with interpersonal relationships. In order to understand the context for various policies that provide structure and boundaries for workplace relationships, one must have a general understanding of human nature so that one can perceive, evaluate, and respond to a variety of situations effectively and appropriately. This chapter examines the nature of human relationships in workplace settings by focusing on three key themes: power, trust, and meaning.

Power

Power can be defined simply as the ability to get things done. There are many forms of power, because there are many ways to do things. There is physical power, intellectual power, and creative power. There is power in beauty, humor, and joy. Speed, cleverness, accuracy, attentiveness, and confidence may all play a role in enhancing one's power.

Businesses, of course, emphasize accomplishing their goals, which requires getting certain things done. Whether a business provides products or services, what it provides, how much, and at what return are important measures of a business's success. That is why expressions like "results-oriented" and "bottom line" are commonplace in the business world. Power is essential for business. A business that has no power, or cannot effectively make use of the power available to it, is soon defunct. Given that power is necessary, along with the fact that power takes many different forms, a key question in business ethics is, what determines whether certain uses of power are ethical or unethical?

To answer that question, it is necessary to look at the different types of power. A widely used and influential description of power comes from the work of two social psychologists, John R.P. French and Bertram Raven. In *The Social Bases of Power*, they describe five basic types of power:

1. Coercive Power: This is the ability to force people to do what one wants them to do. An example is when one person threatens to punish another for doing or failing to do something.

2. Reward Power: This is closely related to coercive power in that it relies on external motivation to get people to do something. Providing payment for services or benefits to employees, setting work schedules, and recognizing an individual as "employee of the month" are all examples of reward power.

3. Legitimate Power: This is the type of power that comes from a person's recognized position within an organization or segment of society. An example of legitimate power would be a small business owner's ability to sell his or her company or to set a new strategic direction.

4. Referent Power: This is power that comes from a person's ability to influence or persuade others. It is dependent both on the leader's character and on the attitude of those who choose to follow. Gandhi is an example of someone who relied upon referent power in leading a movement for political reform largely through the influence of his personal example and speeches.

5. Expert Power: This is a form of power that comes from knowledge or expertise in a certain area. For example, a lawyer who specializes in public construction law might be brought in to advise a developer on how to legally solicit bids for a project on which they are working. In such a case, the lawyer would be exercising expert power.[3]

There are difficulties with French and Raven's taxonomy of power.[4] The five types are not exhaustive. Nor are they exclusive: it is quite common for someone to exercise different types of power, say, legitimate power and reward power, at the same time. But the French and Raven taxonomy provides a good starting point for asking the question, are there some types of power that are inherently problematic from an ethical point of view?

The previous chapter examined four ways of approaching ethical reasoning—using truth, consequences, fairness, and character. Truth allows one to put things in perspective, to observe what is really happening in the appropriate context. Consequences focus on results—allowing one to compare different possible "ends" and determine which ends are important and how important they

---

3. John R.P. French and Bertram Raven, "The Bases of Social Power," in *Studies in Social Power*, ed. Dorwin Cartwright (Ann Arbor: University of Michigan, 1959), 150–67.

4. See Eric Boland, *Clout: Finding and Using Power at Work* (New York: Palgrave Macmillan, 2014), for a discussion of the shortcomings of the French and Raven model.

are. Fairness and character allow one to pay particular attention to the means by which one achieves desired ends. They focus on the "how," not just the "what." Fairness and character are the main types of reasoning one brings to bear when considering the ethical implications of power.

Power and Fairness

When thinking about power from the point of view of fairness, the guiding question becomes, what kinds of power would one *not* want used upon oneself? For most people, there are three types of behavior related to coercive power that are especially unwelcome when one is on the receiving end: force (e.g., physical violence, threats, and intimidation), manipulation (e.g., emotional games, exclusion, and belittlement), and deception (e.g., lack of transparency, misdirection, and lying).

Federal and sometimes state laws prohibit certain forms of coercion such as sexual harassment and racial discrimination. Many workplaces have policies that go even further, protecting workers from additional types of harassment or bullying. Nevertheless, a great deal of abuse of power takes place because it is impossible to define precisely all the ways a person can be acted upon by others that might legitimately be resented. Surveys on workplace bullying suggest that at least one quarter of American workers have experienced some form of harassment or intimidation, most of it unaddressed or unacknowledged by those who could stop it.[5]

Sometimes coercive power is ethically justified, for example, when it is used to protect people from harm.[6] The workplace bully who persistently harasses employees may have to be forcibly removed from the office. The construction worker who endangers others by neglecting to follow safety guidelines may have to be fined or reassigned. But a commitment to fairness should lead one to be suspicious of coercive power, because coercion is used to force people to

---

5. "Office Bullying Plagues Workers across Races, Job Levels and Educational Attainment, According to CareerBuilder's New Study," Career Builder, September 18, 2014, *http://workplacebullying.org/multi/pdf/cb2014survey.pdf*.

6. Immanuel Kant argued that coercion (that is, an act that constrains a person's freedom) is permissible only when it is necessary to protect another person's freedom.

do something they otherwise would not willingly do, while treating other people with respect generally requires one to seek their consent. Even though consent is not always possible, it is presumed to be ethically preferable. Thus, in just about every type of human interaction, noncoercive techniques such as explaining, persuading, or bargaining should be one's first option.

Power and Character

When thinking about power from the point of view of character, the guiding question becomes, how does this use of power affect the kind of person one is or will become? In *The Iliad; or, The Poem of Force*, Simone Weil defines force as the power to turn a person into a thing. Physical coercion violates human nature when it treats a person—a subject (i.e., a creature with a soul, with consciousness)—like an object (i.e., a thing to be manipulated).

> Anybody who is in our vicinity exercises a certain power over us by his very presence, and a power that belongs to him alone, that is, the power of halting, repressing, modifying each movement that our body sketches out. If we step aside for a passer-by on the road, it is not the same thing as stepping aside to avoid a bill-board; alone in our rooms, we get up, walk about, sit down again quite differently from the way we do when we have a visitor. But this indefinable influence that the presence of another human being has on us is not exercised by men whom a moment of impatience can deprive of life, who can die before even thought has a chance to pass sentence on them. In their presence, people move about as if they were not there; they, on their side, running the risk of being reduced to nothing in a single instant, imitate nothingness in their own persons. Pushed, they fall. Fallen, they lie where they are, unless chance gives somebody the idea of raising them up again.[7]

---

7. Simone Weil, *The Iliad; or, The Poem of Force* (Wallingford, PA: Pendle Hill Publications, 1956), 7.

Whereas Immanuel Kant argues that it is morally impermissible to treat another person merely as a means to an end,[8] Weil complements Kant's prohibition by describing what happens to a person treated in such a fashion, especially to someone who is treated that way repeatedly. Consider the number and variety of people who work in contemporary conditions of slavery, including child laborers, sex workers, and victims of sweatshops.[9] And consider also the number of people who have seemingly normal jobs in respectable organizations and yet have no opportunity to voice dissatisfaction without suffering reprisals. To be treated as though one has no voice, no meaningful presence within the organization, is to be deprived of something essential to one's humanity.

But the use of force does more than just harm the victim. As Weil points out, it deprives the person who uses force of his or her humanity as well.

> The man who is the possessor of force seems to walk through a non-resistant element; in the human substance that surrounds him nothing has the power to interpose, between the impulse and the act, the tiny interval that is reflection. . . . Since other people do not impose on their movements that halt, that interval of hesitation, wherein lies all our consideration for our brothers in humanity, they conclude that destiny has given complete license to them, and none at all to their inferiors. And at this point they exceed the measure of the force that is actually at their disposal.[10]

In this passage Weil points out that because having power (or "force") over others removes obstacles to one's actions, and because those obstacles are the very things that frequently cause one to pause and reflect—even if momentarily—on the appropriateness of one's actions, power inhibits ethical reflection. Thus coercive power has a

---

8. See chapter 3.

9. See UNESCO's "Trafficking Statistics Project," at *http://www.unescobkk.org/index.php?id=1022.*

10. Weil, *The Iliad; or, The Poem of Force,* 13–14.

tendency to affect one's character, primarily in regard to the way in which one perceives (or fails to perceive) the full humanity of those around him or her. Therefore, the wise person will employ coercive power judiciously, realizing that its use always comes with a cost.

Persuasion

Early in his career at AT&T, Robert K. Greenleaf discovered that he was often more influential in situations where he held less power. He described observing how often the president of AT&T, Eugene McNeely, was hampered by his institutional authority. He could force people to do what he wanted, but he had a hard time getting people to agree with him, to see things his way.

> Every once in a while I would find myself listening to McNeely talking about a nettling organizational problem, someplace where the outfit was really snafu, and he wouldn't know how to get at it. If, after listening, I felt I understood what he was talking about, I might say, "Gene, would you like for me to get into that and see if I can straighten it out?" And he would say, "Please do." Now, he would never *ask* me to do that because if he asked me, I would be empowered. In other words, I would be seen as his agent; but if I volunteered on my own, then I was on my own. I would have to rely on persuasion.[11]

This might seem counterintuitive. After all, won't people be more inclined to listen to someone they report to rather than to someone who has no authority over them at all? Certainly, in some respects, they would. People might be more inclined to obey or submit to the orders of someone who holds coercive power over them, but they are less inclined to listen fully to a proposal and give internal assent. Greenleaf thought that most leaders rely upon coercive power because it is easier exercise than persuasion, and because of that, they end up losing even the potential of using persuasion effectively.

---

11. Robert K. Greenleaf, cited in Don M. Frick, *Robert K. Greenleaf: A Life of Servant Leadership* (San Francisco: Berrett-Koehler, 2004), 143.

I think if top managers could realize the tremendous liability of holding this power [coercion], and how it really disqualifies them to persuade, they would know they can't be accepted as a persuader. A persuader can't have an axe to grind. This is part of the problem of our structures. We've never thought through what to do with persuasion when you set up a hierarchical structure, and yet many don't know any other way to organize [their structures].[12]

Greenleaf looked upon a commitment to listening and persuasion as an indicator of strong, effective, and ethical leadership. By relying upon persuasion to get others to agree, one tends to pay closer attention to what is really important rather than what is simply urgent. After all, others are much more likely to be persuaded when they can see for themselves that an activity is truly important. Thus the successful use of persuasion requires one "to withdraw and reorient oneself," to get priorities straight in one's own mind. He referred to this process, the deliberate withholding of power in favor of listening, as the "art of systematic neglect."[13] It is necessary, he thought, if a person in a leadership role wants to cultivate the virtue of wisdom, that is, to really perceive and understand what is going on in one's organization.

The Limits of Power

Because power tends to separate decision makers from the effects of their decisions, ethical leaders try to ensure that decisions are routinely made at, or at least genuine input collected from, every organizational level. This practice reflects the conviction that in a healthy organizational culture, every person has something valuable to contribute.[14]

---

12. Ibid., 144.

13. Greenleaf, *The Servant as Leader*, 8.

14. Intentionally limiting one's use of power to promote the common good and, at the same time, to promote the inherent dignity of other people, is known in Catholic social teaching as the "principle of subsidiarity."

Howard Behar, the former president of Starbucks North America, elevates the practice of surrendering power to a leadership principle, calling it: "the person who sweeps the floor should choose the broom":

> Many companies are so bogged down with management and organizational layers that decisions directly affecting the day-to-day of an individual's job are often made without his or her input. Ideally, everyone who will be affected by a particular decision or change should be involved in the process at some level or should have their views taken into consideration. Once everyone has come to an agreement about what needs to be accomplished, then the people with the hands-on expertise can follow through in the most effective way.[15]

It is important to stress that the observations of people like Howard Behar, Robert Greenleaf, and Simone Weil about the use of power are not just anecdotal musings. They are supported by recent empirical research. In a well-known series of contemporary studies of power in organizations, Nathanael Fast, an assistant professor of management and organization at the University of Southern California's Marshall School of Business, empirically confirmed many of the claims made here. Using a variety of research techniques, Fast and his colleagues discovered the following:

- People who have power but do not feel competent are more likely to use bullying tactics on others.[16]
- People who have power but do not have status within an organization are more likely to engage in destructive, demeaning behavior.[17]

---

15. Howard Behar, *It's Not about the Coffee: Leadership Principles from a Life at Starbucks* (New York: Penguin, 2007), 55.

16. Nathanael J. Fast and Serena Chen, "When the Boss Feels Inadequate: Power, Incompetence, and Aggression," *Psychological Science* 20 (2009): 1406–13.

17. Nathanael J. Fast et al., "The Destructive Nature of Power without Status," *Journal of Experimental Social Psychology* 48 (2011): 391–94.

- Power tends to create an illusion of increased control over outcomes, which results in overconfidence and poor decision making.[18]

But it is not enough to point out the dangers of power. The challenge for those who wish to employ ethical forms of influence in organizations is to know what to focus on instead. To that end, the discussion now turns to the cultivation of trust.

Trust

In healthy organizations, healthy societies, and healthy families, people tend to talk *with* one another. In dysfunctional organizations, societies, and families, people are more likely to talk *about* one another. The key difference is the presence or absence of trust. Despite the fact that almost all organizations say they value trust, most organizations struggle to achieve it. Since 1973, the Gallup organization has conducted surveys asking people how much confidence they have in various institutions in American society.

The amount of confidence people express in big business varies from one year to the next, most likely reflecting attitudes shaped by news stories. Yet from 1977 to 2001, the percentage of people expressing a "great deal/quite a lot" of confidence in big business was about the same as those who express "very little/none." After 2001, the ratio changed drastically. In 2002, 32 percent had very little/no confidence in big business compared to 20 percent who had a great deal/quite a lot; by 2015, the percentage of those who expressed very little/no confidence was nearly double those who expressed a great deal/quite a lot of confidence.[19]

The following table, based upon Gallup polling information, represents the percentage of people who expressed "a great deal," "quite a lot," "very little," or "no" confidence in big business.

---

18. Nathanael J. Fast et al., "Illusory Control: A Generative Force behind Power's Far-Reaching Effects," *Psychological Science* 20 (2009): 502–8. See also Nathanael J. Fast et al., "Power and Overconfident Decision-Making," *Organizational Behavior and Human Decision Processes* 117 (2012): 249–60.

19. Gallup Poll, "Big Business," *www.gallup.com/poll/1597/confidence-institutions .aspx.*

GALLUP POLL: CONFIDENCE IN BIG BUSINESS			
	Great Deal	Quite a Lot	Very Little	None
2015	9	12	34	3
2013	9	13	31	2
2011	8	11	34	4
2009	6	10	36	5
2007	7	11	38	3
2005	9	14	29	2
2003	8	14	31	2
2001	10	18	23	3
1999	11	19	24	1
1997	11	17	24	3
1995	8	13	24	2
1993	7	16	28	3
1991	11	15	22	3
1990	9	16	28	3
1988	7	18	26	4
1985	8	24	22	2
1983	7	21	26	2
1981	6	14	29	11
1979	11	21	26	2
1977	11	21	25	2

What happened to undermine Americans' trust in big business? In 2001, Enron, a Houston-based energy company, was found to have purposely misled investors, resulting in criminal convictions of top executives, company bankruptcy, and a loss of $74 billion to shareholders. That scandal was followed by similar accounting frauds at WorldCom and Tyco in 2002. The vast majority of large corporations do not mislead their investors, but trust is highly influenced by perception, and scandals, when they occur, tend to dominate the news. Even though fraud was perpetrated by a relatively small number of businesses, those instances severely affected the trust people had for big business in general.

It only takes a few instances of deception to influence the attitudes of a majority of customers and investors; likewise, a few instances of abuse of power can influence the attitudes of a majority of employees within a company. When those in leadership positions use coercion or manipulation in an attempt to motivate employees, it can be especially difficult to establish trust in the workplace. Sportswriter Jon Bois writes about his experience working as a salesperson at RadioShack:

> At least once a month, often on our days off, we were expected to show up, in dress code, to the district office for a two-hour meeting. Sometimes we'd be individually picked out and shamed as people whose sales numbers weren't good enough for them. I still remember a woman crying in front of everyone and leaving in embarrassment.
>
> We were also shown videos from the corporate office in Fort Worth. One skit stands out in particular. Four of RadioShack's regional executives were sitting at a poker table, "betting" on which of their regions would perform best in Q3.
>
> **Midwest executive:** I'm betting that my region leads sales this quarter.
>
> **Northeast executive:** You know what? My sales associates know they need to offer DirecTV and Sprint to every customer who walks in the door. I will call you . . . and raise you. [shoves stack of chips to middle of table]
>
> **Southwest executive:** Well, my sales associates know they must sell H.O.T. the A.A.A. way! I raise!
>
> **Northwest executive:** When it comes to my sales associates . . . [pushes enormous stack of chips] . . . I'm allllll in.

We were supposed to watch this and take pride in our thousand-store region and be motivated to, I don't know, earn bonuses for these executives? We, the people taking home a thousand bucks a month, who go to work with holes in our last pairs of khakis, who walk an hour to work every day because we can't afford car repairs, who managed a store for 80 hours last week and received a figure below minimum wage for the trouble. We, who are scuttling our only day off so we can sit here and hear about the money they want to make and how useless we are.[20]

People tend to trust those who know them, who are genuinely concerned about their well-being, and who have demonstrated that they will act upon that concern. In his story about RadioShack, Bois portrays regional managers who did not know their employees and were solely concerned about themselves. It is clear what they were trying to accomplish through the video: they wanted to motivate their employees to work harder and increase the numbers by carrying out the plan they had put in place (i.e., offer every customer DirecTV and Sprint). And yet, if that is what they wanted, they would have done much better by trying to gain their salespersons' trust. Forty years of extensive research on trust shows that it improves ethical behavior, performance, retention, job satisfaction, and loyalty to the company.[21] If an organizational leader wants to create a more virtuous, healthier, happier, more productive company, he or she should start by cultivating trust.

Trust and the Virtues

The chief reason many organizations struggle to cultivate trust is that no recipe or strategy is guaranteed to produce it. To be trusted, one must extend trust to others and then be trustworthy oneself over a long period of time. Attempts to instill trust quickly, like through team-building exercises or company retreats, may establish familiarity and thus contribute to a long-term effort to build trust, but they cannot accomplish much in and of themselves. That is because trust results from character; it is not a product of technique. There is no "formula" for trust.

---

20. "A Eulogy for RadioShack, the Panicked and Half-Dead Retail Empire," November 26, 2014, *http://www.sbnation.com/2014/11/26/7281129/radioshack-eulogy-stories*.

21. See Kurt T. Dirks and Daniel P. Skarlicki, "Trust in Leaders: Existing Research and Emerging Issues," in *Trust and Distrust in Organizations: Dilemmas and Approaches*, ed. Roderick M. Kramer and Karen S. Cook (New York: Russell Sage Foundation, 2004), 21–40.

That is not to say there are no practices that predictably enhance—or undermine—trust. There certainly are such practices, and they have an impact on trust because they reveal something significant about the character of those who implement the practices. Consider, for example, the issue of CEO compensation.

In 2013, the CEO-to-worker pay ratio of companies in the S&P 500 was 331:1.[22] (By comparison, the ratio was 46:1 in 1983.) The greatest disparity was at J.C. Penney's, where former CEO Ronald Johnson earned a 2012 compensation package valued at $53.3 million, compared to the average employee wage and benefits of $29,688. That is a 1,795:1 ratio. But it isn't just the size and disparity of the compensation that undermines trust; it is also the fact that CEO pay is rarely linked to performance. Johnson is a prime example. His effort to improve sales by completely remaking the shopping experience at the retail stores confused and alienated the traditional customer base, sales fell precipitously, and the company ended up cutting 43,000 jobs. The six top executives all left J.C. Penney's, but not until they had received a combined $190 million in 2012.[23] The message this sends to employees is that top executives and the board members who approve their compensation packages don't care about the rank and file. Former CEO of Medtronic, Bill George, has long criticized executives and their boards for their lack of character on this issue: "Is it surprising that outsized CEO pay packages destroy employees' trust? With loss of trust, employee motivation gives way to cynicism and superior performance becomes mediocre."[24]

It does not have to be this way, and at many companies it is not. But it takes top leaders with integrity—that is, leaders who exhibit a harmony of wisdom, courage, and temperance—to act contrary to the popular trend of rising CEO compensation.

---

22. "Executive Paywatch," AFL-CIO (2014), *http://edit.aflcio.org/Corporate-Watch/Paywatch-2014.*

23. Elliot Blair Smith and Phil Kuntz, "CEO Pay 1,795-to-1 Multiple of Wages Skirts US Law," *Bloomberg*, April 29, 2013, *http://www.bloomberg.com/news/2013-04-30/ceo-pay-1-795-to-1-multiple-of-workers-skirts-law-as-sec-delays.html.*

24. Bill George, "Nonperforming CEOs," *Business Week*, September 6, 2007, *http://www.businessweek.com/stories/2007-09-06/bill-george-nonperforming-ceosbusinessweek-business-news-stock-market-and-financial-advice.*

Recall the story of Marvin Windows and Doors from chapter 1. Instead of laying off employees during a slump in housing sales, the company reduced workers' hours and cut benefits and then restored them as the economy recovered. CEO Jake Marvin commented, "If we would have cut 1,000 people in early 2009, it would have had a devastating impact on the community."[25] By their actions, the executives at Marvin demonstrated that they cared about the well-being of their employees. And because the company leaders have consistently acted in this way over the years, Marvin Windows and Doors experiences high levels of trust and exceptional performance from its workers.

Trust is an expression of character because it demonstrates integrity. First, trusting behavior—both the tendency to trust others and to be trustworthy—expresses wisdom because it enhances one's understanding of the world, revealing people's inherent goodness.[26] Second, it depends on a commitment to the common good, which precedes the need to satisfy one's own desires (temperance) and is acted upon even in situations of uncertainty or fear (courage). By cultivating trust, a leader in an organization effectively banishes fear, which is often the main motivator of unethical behavior and poor job performance. People who work in an environment free of fear are much more likely to act altruistically, because they are not focused on self-protection.

Trust and Engagement

In 1970, economist Albert O. Hirschman introduced the concepts "voice" and "exit" as ways to describe the two options members of an organization have when experiencing dissatisfaction in the workplace: they can either express their dissatisfaction (voice) or they can leave (exit).[27] And just as there are many ways to voice

---

25. Andrew Martin, "No-Layoff Company Now Writes Profit-Sharing Checks," *New York Times*, December 21, 2012, *http://www.nytimes.com/2012/12/22/business/marvin -windows-and-doors-offers-workers-profit-sharing-checks.html*.

26. See, for example, the study by Nancy Carter and J. Mark Weber showing that people with high levels of generalized trust are more likely to be able to tell when a job candidate is lying. "Not Pollyannas: Higher Generalized Trust Predicts Lie Detection Ability," *Social Psychological and Personality Science* 1 (2010): 274–79.

27. Albert O. Hirschman, *Exit, Voice, and Loyalty: Responses to Decline in Firms, Organizations, and States* (Cambridge, MA: Harvard University Press, 1970).

dissatisfaction—for example, reporting, complaining, recommending, or suggesting—there are also different ways to exit, ranging from leaving the company to staying but refusing to care. In the popular "Dilbert" comic strip, created by Scott Adams, the main character, Dilbert, illustrates voice while his fellow employee Wally, who tries hard to avoid doing any work, illustrates exit. Dilbert is engaged; Wally is disengaged.

Dilbert and Wally represent two different attitudes toward workplace engagement: voice and exit.

An engaged employee is not necessarily always doing the right things, but for the most part, she cares; she wants things to be better than they are in some respect. By contrast, the disengaged employee has opted out and no longer provides any reasons. Like the Herman Melville character Bartleby the Scrivener, he "would prefer not to."[28] So for an ethical culture to develop, an organization must have a sizable portion of engaged members. That is, it must be made up of people who care and are willing to provide reasons why things should be one way or another. That is the only way ethical improvement can take place.

Unfortunately, engaged workers are in the minority. According to the most recent Gallup survey on the state of the American workplace, only 30 percent of workers report feeling "engaged," 52 percent are "not engaged," and 18 percent are "actively disengaged."[29]

---

28. Bartleby is a character in Melville's short story, "Bartleby, the Scrivener: A Story of Wall Street." Whenever his employer asks him to undertake some new task, Bartleby replies simply, "I would prefer not to."

29. "State of the American Workplace: Employee Engagement Insights for US Business Leaders," Gallup, 2013, *http://www.gallup.com/services/178514/state-american-workplace.aspx.*

Voice does not, by itself, generate trust, which is perhaps part of the reason that, while 30 percent of workers report being "engaged," only 22 percent report being both "engaged" and "thriving." After all, people often use voice to create or exacerbate conflict. Still, voice is essential because trust cannot grow in an organization in which people are disengaged.

Eliciting voice requires the habit of active listening, which is paying close attention to what people are saying, feeling, and doing. Robert Greenleaf observed,

> [While listening,] there is an awareness of the growth problems of individuals and the rhythm of growth— ascents, plateaus, declines. There needs to be awareness of what is not being said as well as what is being said. Awareness of feeling-tone is very important. Undercurrents of feeling need to be sensed. Someone may have a feeling of urgency about a problem or an idea, and he may not be expressing it except by subtle signs. These must be seen and understood.[30]

Listening in this way requires the virtue of humility on the part of the listener. Listeners must be able to put aside their own concerns, hopes, fears, insecurities, and focus intently on the other person. Such humility comes only from great confidence. And even though that might seem to be a contradiction, it is not. Confidence means, literally, "faith together"; it is a kind of assuredness that develops in the context of a community of people who rely upon and look out for one another. Those who lack humility nearly always lack confidence as well. It is what makes them overly concerned with their own image and status. As a result, they try to inhibit voice because they fear criticism.[31]

---

30. Robert Greenleaf, "Growth through Groups," cited in Frick, *Robert K. Greenleaf*, 166.

31. "Managers with low managerial self-efficacy (that is, low perceived ability to meet the elevated competence expectations associated with managerial roles) seek to minimize voice as a way of compensating for a threatened ego." Nathanael J. Fast et al., "Managing to Stay in the Dark: Managerial Self-Efficacy, Ego Defensiveness, and the Aversion to Employee Voice," *Academy of Management Journal* 57 (2014): 113–34.

Listening also requires the willingness to forgive. Those who hold power inevitably hurt the people over whom they hold that power. Whether intentionally or unintentionally, through action or inaction, misunderstandings arise, agreements are broken, people are slighted, deceived, abused, or neglected. Listening brings the harms to light. Perhaps the owner of a company is a kind and gracious soul, but the person she hires to run day-to-day operations is a manipulative bully, who ingratiates himself to the owner but is ruthless toward employees. Listening will bring such conduct out, and the owner will be faced with accepting responsibility and seeking forgiveness. Sincerely acknowledging that others have suffered because of one's actions is the greatest burden of leadership. It takes courage.

Hannah Arendt remarked that there are two practices necessary in any society: promising and forgiving. Promising is necessary to bring people together; it is the agreement, whether explicit or implicit, that allows people to come together for some shared purpose. Forgiving is necessary because the promises that bring people together are inevitably broken. In order for a group of people to move forward, for them to become reengaged in shared work, relationships must be restored and new promises entered into. That begins with forgiveness.

Organizations are rarely in the position of simply building trust; usually they are rebuilding trust. Even people new to the organization bring their past experiences with them.

> Why don't I trust corporate leadership? Experience!
>
> At twenty-one I was an administrative assistant to a CEO of a large Minnesota business. The face he gave the world was charming and charismatic. In the office, he was an angry, screaming narcissist who often berated employees in front of everyone. He would call me into his boardroom, have me lock the door, and rub his back—sometimes for up to four hours at a time. I was a kid, I didn't know how to say no to a powerful CEO. I was terrified.
>
> After I quit that job, my next gig was with a CEO who chain smoked in the office and treated employees more like prison inmates.[32]

---

32. "Jess," in the comments section of "The State of Minnesota Business Ethics," *MPR News*, November 19, 2014, *http://www.mprnews.org/story/2014/11/19 /daily-circuit-business-ethics*.

Early experiences tend to shape lifelong attitudes. That is true of families, and it is true of businesses as well. For most people, their attitude about business ethics is largely determined by their first significant job. Unless that attitude is reshaped by formative experiences later in life, it will persist throughout many changes in circumstance. Listening and forgiving are crucial steps in reshaping experience so that trust becomes possible once again.

Meaning

To create and maintain a trusting work environment, one that does not rely solely upon coercive strategies to motivate employees but instead uses intrinsic motivations, leaders must understand why people work in the first place. The answer may seem obvious. People work out of necessity—to survive and to pay for food, shelter, and clothing.

For many people in the world, and throughout world history, that is the complete answer. Work is a necessity, and it consists largely of drudgery. That is why work is frequently described in terms like *toil, labor, exertion, effort, elbow grease*, or *blood, sweat, and tears.*

And yet, for most people today who live in the industrialized world, especially those who are educated and have some choice in where to work and what type of work to do, the answer is not so simple. If work is not an activity born solely out of necessity, then what else is it?

Most people want their work to be meaningful in some respect. When people introduce themselves by describing what they do, whether by title, profession, or trade, they are implying that their identity is somehow constituted by their working lives. Who they are is, in some respect, what they do. And this means that to take pride in oneself one must also take pride in one's work. To take pride in something is to regard it as good in some respect and to see one's relationship to it as significant. When people regard their work as essential to producing something good, they tend to find it fulfilling.

In a classic study on workplace motivation, Frederick Herzberg discovered the three things that motivate employees more than anything else are (1) interesting work, (2) challenges, and (3) increased responsibility.[33] This runs counter to what most managers believe motivates their employees. When managers are surveyed, they tend to think that what matters most to their employees is getting recognized for their contributions or receiving support. But workers themselves overwhelming indicate that what matters most to them—that is, what contributes most to their positive mood—is making progress on some significant task or project.[34]

For many people, however, meaningful work remains elusive. Work is neither pure drudgery nor is it fulfilling. It is just something that consumes time and energy.

Here is a sample of a conversation between a college student and her academic advisor:

Student: Dr. Jones, I need to schedule all my classes in the afternoon next semester. I had to pick up a new part-time job and most of the shifts are late at night. I won't be able to get up for early classes.

Advisor: That might be hard to arrange. Do you really have to work two jobs?

Student: Well, I have to make my car payments.

Advisor: I thought you lived on campus. Why do you need a car?

Student: That's the only way I can get to work.

This particular student's reasoning forms a vicious circle that is easy to spot, but it is not so different from people who enmesh themselves in a cycle of indebtedness to support a lifestyle for which work becomes a necessity. In this way, work can become not an integral part of one's chosen life, but merely what one does to support a life conceived as existing separately, apart from work. And the rest of one's life becomes what one does either to support one's work or to get away from work. The question of whether one's work is meaningful can come to seem superfluous.

33. Frederick Herzberg, *One More Time: How Do You Motivate Employees?* Boston: Harvard Business Press, 2008.

34. See Teresa Amabile and Steven J. Kramer, "The Power of Small Wins," *Harvard Business Review* 89, no. 5 (May 2011), *https://hbr.org/2011/05/the-power-of-small-wins#*.

One of the common effects of losing sight of work's purpose is burnout. It is a feeling that one's work is pointless, that extra effort does not make any difference, that life as a whole, and especially one's work life, is exhausting and unrelenting. Under such conditions, an ethical culture is difficult to maintain because people become dispirited and disengaged, more willing to ignore bad behavior from coworkers, more likely to lower standards when it comes to their own conduct.

Work–Life Balance

American full-time employees spend an average of 1,700 hours per year on the job. That is significantly more than Germans, who spend an average of 1,400 hours working, and much less than Greek workers, who spend 2,000 hours per year at work.[35] Surprisingly, the hours spent at work do not correspond to productivity. German productivity is 70 percent higher than Greek.[36]

Burnout is generally thought to come from working too much. Sometimes, of course, working too much causes serious problems, as in the case of Julie Thao, a nurse who mistakenly gave her patient an intravenous anesthetic rather than antibiotics. The patient died, and Thao was charged with a felony. It was a serious error, caused at least in part because Thao had worked a sixteen hour shift the day before and then slept at the hospital in order to get up early and start another shift the day of the incident.[37] Stories like this are often cited as examples of burnout, and yet Thao was more physically than mentally exhausted. Even a person who finds her work fulfilling is prone to mistakes when severely deprived of sleep.

Burnout describes a condition more complex than simply working too much. It refers to an exhaustion that comes from doing the wrong kind of work, working with the wrong people, or going to

---

35. Joe Weisenthal, "Check Out How Much the Average American Works Each Year Compared to the French, the Germans, and the Koreans," August 17, 2013, *http://www.businessinsider.com/average-annual-hours-worked-for-americans-vs-the-rest-of-the-world-2013-8#ixzz3MHufgf3K.*

36. "This Chart Shows the Relationship between Hours Worked and Productivity," *Economist*, October 6, 2013, *http://www.businessinsider.com/the-relationship-between-hours-worked-and-productivity-2013-10.*

37. "Nurse Charged with Felony in Fatal Medical Error," *Medical Ethics Advisor* 23, no. 2 (2007): 20.

work with the wrong type of motivation. The suggested remedy of spending less time at work in order to balance the work–life scale, therefore, is bound to be ineffective since it does not address the need for finding work that is meaningful in the first place.

The phrase "work–life balance" is a misnomer. It is not as if there is "work" on one side of the scale and "life" on the other side. What one needs, instead, is "balance in life," a steady diet of activity that is meaningful and life-giving to balance the necessary but tedious activities that are repetitive, dull, and energy-draining. Such activities are not confined to the workplace. Many household chores, like washing dishes, mowing the lawn, or paying bills, can be just as depleting as workplace activities.

It is important to note that activities can be energy-draining even if one finds them enjoyable. Watching television, for instance, is something many people enjoy doing when they are not working, but it tends to leave people feeling emotionally and physically drained if they do it too much. In contrast, many forms of exercise are tedious, yet one feels refreshed after doing them.

What kinds of activities give a person energy? The particulars differ considerably from one person to another, but the general characteristics are as follows:

- Meaningful—contributing to something worthwhile
- Creative—making or transforming into something new and valuable
- Relational—deepening one's relationships with others

Language itself is partly to blame for confusion about the relative value of leisure activities. Words that are used to denote not working are generally associated with doing nothing, hence expressions like "weekend," "vacation," "time off," "retirement," all of which imply emptiness or negation. But just as work must have meaning to be part of a fulfilling life, time away from work must be meaningful, too. If one's time away from work is not used wisely, then the weekend becomes just another part of a series of "one damn thing after another"[38] that actually contributes to burnout instead of preventing it.

---

38. "Life is just one damn thing after another" is a well-known saying usually attributed to Elbert Hubbard, an American writer and champion of the arts and crafts movement.

Circles of Life

The term *work–life balance* sets up false opposition; if you care about your work it is part of your life.

Attempts to balance work versus life puts one on a teeter-totter, creating imbalance.

If you try to cram everything that is fun or interesting into weekends, vacation, or retirement, you are not creating a full, coherent, and integrated life.

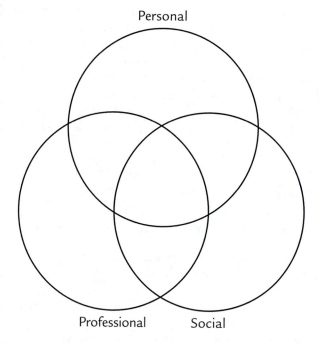

Personal

Professional   Social

Write down all your regular activities in the appropriate circles. The things that give you positive energy are the things that give you meaning and joy in your life. Some things that you enjoy

Continued

Circles of Life Continued

doing, like playing video games or social networking, may deprive you of energy. It varies from one person to another.

Activities that overlap should be written in the middle. For example, volunteering at a local animal shelter or a church may give you energy, and touch your personal, professional, and social circles.

Avoid activities that drain your energy and don't contribute in a positive way to the story of your life.

Don't worry about having the same number of items in each circle. Instead, note whether the positives outweigh the negatives.

The ancient Greeks spoke of *scholē*, generally translated as "leisure," from which we get the term "school." Whereas people today tend to think the purpose of schools (and universities) is to prepare young people for work, the ancient Greeks thought of work as what one did in order to have leisure, including, but not limited to, going to school.[39]

Organizational Hero
LINDON "LINDY" SALINE

Successful careers do not start with employment, they start much earlier: in childhood. Lindy Saline's career was no exception. From his active involvement with a neighborhood church, the Boy Scouts, and Hi-Y (a YMCA-sponsored youth group), Lindy developed both an interest in and a talent for civic engagement, as well as a set of leadership skills that would serve him throughout a long, successful career at General Electric.

Continued

---

39. See Josef Pieper, *Leisure: The Basis of Culture* (South Bend, IN: St. Augustine's Press, 1998).

Organizational Hero: LINDON "LINDY" SALINE *Continued*

An electrical engineer by training, Lindy advanced quickly at GE—from managing small projects to managing teams of people. In the fall of 1962, he was asked to lead a team of more than eight hundred engineers to Cape Canaveral, Florida, to implement the integrated launch control and checkout system for the Apollo program. The engineering was one challenge, but Lindy soon found he faced another challenge, one that wasn't included in his job description: making sure that the families of his engineering team could successfully integrate into Volusia County.

At that time, the population of Volusia County was approximately 130,000 people. The largest city was Daytona Beach, occupied mainly by retirees and tourists. The interior part of the county was agricultural. In addition, education was not a priority in that part of the country. Not only were the school buildings inadequate, but the public school system as a whole was not performing up to the educational standards expected by professionals from upstate New York.

Lindy put together a team of volunteers to look into what could be done about improving the schools. They called themselves the "Task Force for Tax Reform." Their purpose: increase taxes to fund the schools. As they looked into the situation, they discovered that property in Florida was assessed at an average of only 20–25 percent of the market value, in violation of state law requiring assessed value to match market value. To remedy the situation, the task force set forth a four-step strategy:

1. Inform the public of the situation.
2. Approach the County Commissioners and inform them of their duty to implement proper assessments.
3. Provide the commissioners with a schedule for implementation.
4. File a lawsuit against the commissioners if they did not implement the assessments in accordance with the schedule.

The first part of the strategy was key, and for the next several months, Lindy spent most evenings on the road, speaking to

Continued

Organizational Hero: LINDON "LINDY" SALINE *Continued*

civic groups throughout the county, trying to win public support. The effort was exhausting for Lindy and his family. Taking a public stand on an unpopular issue meant constant scrutiny. His children saw his face more often on the television news and in the newspaper than at home, and they had to endure frequent threatening telephone calls. It was not unusual for Lindy to be accosted in a parking lot after a presentation.

The County Commissioners failed to follow through with the revised assessments, so the task force filed suit, and the decision ultimately went before the Florida Supreme Court. *Saline et al. v. County Commissioners* was decided in favor of the task force and helped to secure better funding for Florida schools for years to come.

Not only did Lindy's family bear much of the emotional burden of getting the tax reform approved, they never benefitted from the results of his efforts. By the time new school funding went into effect, Lindy had been reassigned to New York, this time to head the GE Management Development Institute in Crotonville. Over the next twelve years, he would be responsible for training five thousand employees a year, including many of those in senior leadership positions at GE today.

Lindy has been retired now for many years, but retirement, for him, is just an opportunity for a different kind of work. Putting the skills he learned from the Management Institute to work, he has led more than fifty nonprofit organizations through strategic planning.

For Lindy, leading ethically is principally a matter of integrity, which requires a commitment to doing good work in one's civic life as well as one's professional career, taking care of the present and looking out for the future.

The Role of Friendship in Meaningful Work

Near the end of the *Nicomachean Ethics*, after discussing the nature of happiness and describing each of the major virtues, Aristotle devotes two chapters to the topic of friendship. To contemporary readers, this may seem an odd choice. After all, what does friendship have to do with ethics? And it may have seemed an odd choice to Aristotle's contemporaries as well, for he begins by explaining why it is important:

> After what we have said, a discussion of friendship would naturally follow, since it is a virtue or implies virtue, and is besides most necessary with a view to living. For without friends no one would choose to live, though he had all other goods; even rich men and those in possession of office and of dominating power are thought to need friends most of all; for what is the use of such prosperity without the opportunity of beneficence, which is exercised chiefly and in its most laudable form towards friends? . . . Friendship seems too to hold states together, and lawgivers seem to care more for it than for justice; for unanimity seems to be something like friendship, and this they aim at most of all, and expel faction as their worst enemy; and when men are friends they have no need of justice, while when they are just they need friendship as well, and the truest form of justice is thought to be a friendly quality.[40]

Friendship, says Aristotle, is what holds organizations together. Evidence of workplace engagement certainly seems to support that claim. In *Vital Friends*, Tom Rath reports that people who have a "best friend" at work are seven times more likely to be engaged in their job.[41] People who have friends at work are more likely to enjoy spending time there, to share ideas, to help each other out, and to do all the little things that make successful companies more productive.

But friendship also poses dangers. Despite Aristotle's claim that friends "have no need of justice," it is actually the very closeness produced by friendship that necessitates laws and policies to prevent harm to those outside the circle of friendship. Friends can be exclusive, creating intimacy among themselves but making life difficult

---

40. Aristotle, *Nicomachean Ethics* 8.1, trans. C.D.C. Reeve (Indianapolis: Hackett, 2014).

41. Tom Rath, *Vital Friends: The People You Can't Afford to Live Without* (New York: Gallup, 2005).

for the newcomer or the outsider. Friendship can lead to partiality or bias. For that reason, many companies have policies on employee dating, especially between supervisors and subordinates. Such policies establish boundaries intended to reduce subtle forms of coercion or the influence of favoritism. Other forms of favoritism, such as nepotism, are prohibited in many workplaces, especially public organizations. Discrimination can also be a form of favoritism, when choices about hiring or promotion are influenced by the feeling that one "feels more comfortable with" members of a certain race, age, or gender. Policies on sexual harassment are needed to prevent some people from seeking unwelcome or unreciprocated intimacy.

This is where practical wisdom is needed to steer a course between the Scylla of unrestrained favoritism and the Charybdis of a sterile, antisocial workplace.[42] The ethical business is one that encourages close, productive relationships that contribute to a positive work environment while discouraging forms of favoritism and unwelcome advances that contribute to a dysfunctional or hostile environment. The operative virtue in such a workplace is reverence. In a reverent community, each person regards others as bearers of inherent dignity and worth. Reverence imposes upon each person an obligation to treat others with humility, charity, and respect. Respecting the dignity of others is always challenging, even for those who wield power conscientiously, with the best intentions.

A scene in the movie *A River Runs Through It*, in which Paul Maclean, the younger son, refuses to eat his oatmeal, beautifully illustrates the difficulty of negotiating relationships in which intimacy and power are combined—as in leader and follower or father and son.[43] Paul's father refuses to excuse him from the table, and so Paul sits there impassively, all day long, defying his father, neither of them willing to give in to the other. The scene foreshadows the tragedy that is to befall the family later in the story. The struggle is characteristic of a drama played out over and over in families and organizations where one person has authority over another and the subordinate, for one reason or another, refuses to acknowledge the terms of that authority.

---

42. Scylla and Charybdis were two sea monsters from Greek mythology between which sailors had to steer their ships.

43. The movie is based on the novella by Norman Maclean.

Commenting on this scene, author David James Duncan writes, "For all the love and admirable qualities of the father, it was, one felt, his dogmatic stance that prevented grace from flowing in the son."[44]

Who knows what drama played out in the father's own childhood decades earlier; whether the willfulness that he sought to subdue in his son—for his son's own well-being—is not the same willfulness that had been so long restrained in himself by strict adherence to the rules of the household. Yet it is those very rules, or perhaps his insistence on them, or his manner of insisting on them, that creates a wall separating him from his son.

Friendships are relationships characterized by mutual flourishing. And every organization, whether it is a family, a small business, or a large corporation, is made healthy and whole when the human potential of its members finds fuller expression through their participation. But wholeness and health are not always possible. Sometimes leaders are required to do what they can to prevent harm, to establish and enforce rules, policies, and procedures intended to ensure everyone's safety and well-being, while knowing that the cost of such an exercise of power may inhibit others from flourishing.

Conclusion

No matter what kind of organization in which one works, or what kind of role one has within it, the most significant ethical challenges almost always involve negotiating the use of power while preserving good relationships among the people with whom one interacts. More often than not, this requires the willingness to forgo the use of some forms of power that would otherwise be at hand. Such willingness is illustrated by Jerry Arndt, a former executive at Trane, a manufacturing company specializing in heating, ventilation, and air conditioning systems:

> My job at Trane was my first job out of college. I started as a manufacturing engineer. After a brief orientation I was given an assignment that initially looked impossible and

---

44. Duncan attributes this observation to Henry Bugbee, a philosophy professor at the University of Montana, whom he heard discussing the movie during a radio interview. David James Duncan, "Five Henry Stories," in *Wilderness and the Heart: Henry Bugbee's Philosophy of Place, Presence, and Memory*, ed. Edward F. Mooney (Athens: University of Georgia Press, 1999), 248.

overwhelming to me. I really didn't have a clue. It was a technology project that didn't lend itself to finding more experienced engineers that could help me. After struggling for a few days, it dawned on me that the people in the factory might be able to help me. They really understood the existing processes that this new technology would replace. I asked the folks in that factory department if they would be willing to let me join them for lunch in the factory lunch room for a few days to chat about my project and whether they would be willing to give me some advice and guidance. I think they expected to hear from some new hotshot engineer about what I would be doing to them and how their lives would change. Instead, what they saw was a sincere and genuine call for help. They were awesome. The project was a big success. It was because of them and they got the credit. When I left Trane after almost thirty-five years, somebody reflected on that experience during the comments at my Trane farewell party. That experience in my first two weeks of a thirty-five-year career stuck in my mind and in the minds of others that were involved.[45]

It is only through the renunciation of power, traditionally conceived, that genuine trust can be established in relationships. When the leader performs a sincere act of hospitality, by humbling herself and treating the others as guests, all suggestion that the others have only instrumental value is abolished. The people served are valuable for their own sake. Their contributions are significant. They have dignity. They are able to meet one another in a shared recognition without the skepticism that inevitably accompanies arrangements of rank. Trust is the glue that bonds relationships together. It makes a "we" out of two "I's" united by shared meaning. Thus welcomed into the organization, together they become part of its deep story.

Discussion Questions

1. What kinds of power do you have within your organization? What kinds of power do you have among your friends?

---

45. Jerry Arndt, e-mail message to author, April 24, 2015.

2. Do you think you are a good listener? What would your friends or coworkers say about your listening abilities?

3. What is your trust tolerance? Is it more important for you to trust others or to make sure that no one takes advantage of you?

4. Do you find your work meaningful? What might you do to make it more meaningful?

Resources for Further Exploration

PRINT

Galinsky, Adam D., Derek D. Rucker, and Joe C. Magee, eds. "Power: Past Findings, Present Considerations, and Future Directions." In *APA Handbook of Personality and Social Psychology*. Vol. 3, *Interpersonal Relations*, edited by Mario Mikulincer and Phillip R. Shaver, 421–60. Washington, DC: American Psychological Association, 2015.

> This essay is a good place to begin when looking at the current state of scholarship on the topic of power.

Hirschman, Albert O. *Exit, Voice, and Loyalty: Responses to Decline in Firms, Organizations and States*. Cambridge, MA: Harvard University Press, 1970.

> Hirschman's classic work on responses to disappointment is still timely and repays close study.

Hurley, Robert F., *The Decision to Trust: How Leaders Create High-Trust Organizations*. Hoboken, NJ: Wiley, 2011.

> This book, by a professor of management at Fordham University, offers a helpful model for understanding how trust functions in organizations.

OTHER MEDIA

Grant, Adam. "Always Wear Dark Suits." TEDx video. July 2011. *http://tedxtalks.ted.com/video/TEDxPhiladelphiaED-Adam -Grant-A*. Time: 00:14:14.

> The author of *Give and Take: Why Helping Others Drives Our Success* (New York: Penguin, 2014) offers an entertaining and insightful TEDx lecture exploring the ways meaningful work reduces burnout.

CHAPTER 4

Ethical Decision Making

Mark Pettigrew is a supervisor at a large manufacturing facility.[1] One evening he received the following e-mail with a photograph attached:

> From: Welder Utility
> Sent: Tuesday, November 05, 2013 7:09 PM
> To: Mark Pettigrew
> Subject: Safety Issue: Falling Light
>
> The light fell in C-24. Just missed a guy that was walking out of his booth.

A large fluorescent light fixture that has just fallen from the ceiling.

---

1. This case is based on an actual incident. People's names and some minor details have been altered.

At first glance, this situation may not seem to require ethical decision making. After all, it is a fairly straightforward safety issue. It does not raise any questions about the sorts of things covered in the employee handbook under "Code of Ethical Behavior"; there is nothing in the e-mail about theft, misrepresentation, or conflict of interest. The situation is serious, but it is just one of many that Mark has to deal with on a regular basis. And yet, upon further consideration, it requires ethical decision making in the same way that many daily situations require such thinking. It presents a situation in which Mark has to work out, with others, the best response. And there are many ways he could respond, some better and some worse, with significant effects on employees' well-being and trust in one another.

Upon receiving the message, Mark contacts Robert, the head of maintenance at the plant, and arranges a meeting first thing in the morning. At the meeting, Robert fills Mark in on the details: "The fixture was installed without lock nuts. A fan located near the light caused vibration, which over time loosened the nuts, and that caused the fixture to fall. We inspected the other fixtures in the surrounding area, and they are fine. I'm confident this was an isolated incident." Mark isn't so sure. If the light fixture had fallen on an employee, he or she could have been seriously injured or even killed. But he understands Robert's reluctance to inspect all the fixtures if it is not necessary. The ceiling is two stories high, requiring a man lift to gain access for inspection. Because of the layout of the workstations, the lift cannot easily be moved from one place to another. It would take a crew of workers the better part of a week to inspect all seven hundred fixtures in the plant. And Robert's crew is already far behind on work orders. How should Mark handle this situation? What is the right thing to do?

Despite first appearances, this is a prime example of an ethical crisis. It is not a crisis in the sense that somebody has, or is about to, commit an egregious moral violation. Rather, it is a crisis in the sense that it presents a very serious situation that demands an immediate response, and how Mark responds to the situation is critical to the well-being of the organization. If nothing is done, more lights may fall from the ceiling, with potentially grave consequences. But if he acts precipitously, without regard to Robert's judgment, he risks damaging his relationship with Robert and his crew, potentially losing credibility in the plant with others upon whom he depends to do his job effectively. When it comes to ethical decision making, knowing what to do and knowing how to do it are equally important, and both require preparation so that one can act appropriately and effectively in the event of a serious situation.

Crisis preparation is something that members of certain professions do on a regular basis. Upon checking into a hotel, the average person will likely notice several things: the carpeting, wall coverings, lighting, decorations, and general cleanliness. But a firefighter, even while on vacation, will most likely notice something the average person would overlook: the location of emergency exits and the number of doorways between her room and the nearest exit. She will notice because she has been trained to find escape routes when her vision is obscured by smoke. Thinking about what to do in the event of a fire emergency is habitual for firefighters; it is something they do automatically. Developing such habits is part of what it means to prepare for a crisis.

People who work in any kind of an organization need to prepare for crises, especially those in leadership roles. But organizational crises are not just physical or financial, they are often ethical. That is, they consist of times when people have serious questions and often disagreements about how to act appropriately. In such situations, the right thing to do may not be obvious; people's vision may be obscured by strong emotions, lack of crucial information, or limited time to make decisions. Nevertheless, decisions must be made. But how does one prepare for the broad range of situations in which appropriate action is not easy to discern and carries with it a range of potential or certain consequences?

This is where training in ethical decision making can be useful. It consists of the following:

1. Training in how to think clearly and consistently in difficult and confusing circumstances so that one can develop the habit of sound practical judgment

2. Training in how to engage others in constructive conversation about what to do

Part of deciding *what* to do is deciding *how* to do it. Thus, in addition to thinking about whether all the light fixtures in the plant should be inspected, Mark also needs to think about how he can engage Robert in the decision-making process. As a leader in the organization, Mark has a responsibility to guide others in an ethically responsible fashion. Otherwise, even though he himself may be able to figure out the most ethically responsible course of action, he might be unable to persuade others to follow that course of action in a thorough and timely fashion.

For one who has a leadership role in an organization, ethics is not simply a matter of determining for oneself what is right and wrong. It is, in addition, a matter of helping others to reach consensus about a common good. To be a good leader, one must also be a teacher. And to be a teacher of the common good, one must understand how ethical reasoning works.

How Ethical Reasoning Works

Most people—including everybody who has the ability to read this book—are experts in ethical reasoning.

The psychologist K. Anders Ericsson has conducted numerous studies on how long it takes someone to become proficient at a certain skill. Repeatedly, in areas ranging from musical performance to basketball to chess, it turns out that ten thousand hours of practice is the threshold for expertise.[2] That doesn't mean, of course, that everyone who practices something for ten thousand hours develops at the same rate or to the same extent, but there does seem to be something significant that happens in brain functioning after a sufficient amount of time has been invested in repeated activity. The activity starts to become second nature. Performing a task that requires great effort and attention for a novice—if it can be done at all—is done effortlessly by the expert.

Parents and teachers introduce ethical reasoning as soon as their children are able to speak in sentences. They ask children to evaluate whether they are telling the truth: "Is that what *really* happened? Tell me the truth." They ask them to think about the consequences of their actions: "What did you think would happen when you pulled the cat's tail?" They ask children to put themselves imaginatively in

---

2. See Malcolm Gladwell, *Outliers: The Story of Success* (New York: Little, Brown and Company, 2008), for a lengthy discussion of Ericsson's "ten-thousand-hour rule."

another's situation: "How would you feel if Juanita ate *your* candy?" They make observations about the character of the child's behavior: "That was really generous of you to share like that," or, "You shouldn't say such mean things to your friends. No one likes a bully."

Talking (and thinking about) how to act, how to treat others, what to do, what not to do, when, where, and under what circumstances, is a constant part of one's daily dialogue, both with others and internally, from age three until the end of one's life. By the time one is twenty years old, one has had more than one hundred thousand hours of practice in ethical reasoning. The typical college-age student is not only good at ethical reasoning, he or she is an expert at it and has indeed been using ethical reasoning at a highly proficient level for many years. It has become second nature. He or she can do it without intentionally thinking about doing it. Most of the time, it is effortless.

Generally speaking, when people talk about ethics, they are drawing attention to situations in which it is not obvious whether a certain action is right or wrong or to situations in which there is considerable disagreement about how to act. That leads people to assume that ethics are mainly about conceptually complex or controversial issues. But most situations about which people make moral evaluations fall into the category of "obviously" right or wrong, good or bad. These include such things as stealing a neighbor's bicycle, showing appreciation for a favor, helping a friend in need, cheating on an exam, punching an innocent stranger in the nose, making false claims on a résumé, betraying a partner, or donating to a worthwhile charity. Actions such as these are typically nonproblematic—that is, they do not require a great deal of thought to determine whether they are morally good or bad. Consider also the many actions that usually fall into the category of morally neutral, such as eating breakfast in the morning, brushing one's teeth, reading a book in the evening, and taking the dog for a walk. Any one of these actions could, of course, be regarded as morally problematic in certain circumstances. Imagine a friend observing each of these listed actions and making a moral judgment: "I can't believe you are eating eggs. Do you realize how cruelly the poultry industry treats chickens?" Or, "You use all-natural toothpaste also! Good for you. I always try to purchase environmentally responsible products." Or, "Why do you read such trash? That author is so sexist!" Or, "It's about time you took your dog for a walk!"

The point here is that ethical evaluation is being done all the time, with regard to all kinds of behavior, and people can move quite easily from implicit, habitual modes of evaluation to intensive, explicit, ethical scrutiny. Nevertheless, only a small percentage of one's daily actions is subject to the kind of intensive, explicit scrutiny that is normally considered to be moral or ethical reasoning.

To see just how common the implicit form of ethical reasoning is—taking place almost continually just below the surface of conscious recognition—consider the following example:

Tim is playing a game of pickup basketball with a group of friends. As he drives the lane, Todd (a member of the opposing team) reaches in and tries to strip the ball. He misses and instead slaps Tim on the wrist. In a game like this, there are no referees, so it is customary for players to call fouls on themselves, if they think it is warranted. In the space of one or two seconds, Todd evaluates whether he should shout, "FOUL!" How does that evaluation proceed? Well, it could include one or more (possibly all) of the following considerations:

- How hard did he slap Tim? Was it hard enough to constitute the sort of thing normally called a foul, or was it the sort of thing normally considered incidental contact?

- Did it result in a disadvantage for the other team? Did Tim continue to the basket and make a layup, or did he lose control of the ball, resulting in a turnover?

- If an opposing player hit him on the arm in the same way under similar circumstances, would he expect the other player to call a foul?

- Ward never calls fouls on himself, no matter how hard he hits another player. No one can stand playing with Ward, and Todd doesn't want to be like that. If he does not call a foul, would he be acting like Ward?

Notice that the four types of considerations that occur to Todd correspond to the four modes of ethical evaluation that children learn at an early age: truth, consequences, fairness, and character. Notice also that Todd does not have to stop playing in order to consider these things. They just go through his mind in a split second. (It takes much longer to read them than for Todd to think them.) That is because Todd is an expert ethical reasoner. He is simply doing what he has been doing every hour of every day since he first learned how to think about such things. He does not even pause to consider that he is engaging in ethical reasoning. It is just what he does.

The ease with which human beings make implicit ethical evaluations is both a blessing and curse. The blessing is that one does not have to stop to think carefully about every action. If that were necessary, one would hardly be able to do anything at all. But as it is, one can carry on a constant stream of ethical reasoning while doing many other things without interruption, in the same way that one can eat french fries while reading a book or have a conversation while walking with a friend. The curse is that on those occasions when ethically problematic situations arise, it can be difficult to step out of the implicit, habitual mode of reasoning and think carefully and consistently about what is right and wrong.

Detecting the operation of intuitive moral judgments in oneself is fairly easy. One simply has to read the headlines of the "Letters to the Editor" from any newspaper. Take the following headlines, published recently in various newspapers:

"Single-Payer Would Provide Better Health Care to More People," *St. Louis Post-Dispatch*

"Digital Billboards: A Bad Idea," *Sacramento Bee*

"Why Wait on Minimum Wage?" *Journal Star*

"Courtesy Says We Should Clean Up after Ourselves," *Des Moines Register*

It is practically impossible to read the headlines without feeling oneself already inclined to agree or disagree with each of the letter writers, despite having no idea whether the writers actually provide a coherent argument. One can easily supply a number of reasons supporting one's inclinations. There is no need to wait for the writer's argument to decide whether one agrees or disagrees; the reader can supply his or her own reasons.

Why is this problematic? Well, for one thing, it illustrates the extent to which people tend to choose sides in disputes before they have taken time to consider carefully the merits and demerits of their position. Personal interests, loyalties, fears, desires, and formative experiences all play a role in determining one's inclinations. And because people are so adept at ethical reasoning, they can easily find reasons supporting what they like. This all takes place at a subconscious level—quickly, easily, without paying much attention to what one is doing.

In *The Righteous Mind: Why Good People Are Divided by Politics and Religion*, Jonathan Haidt uses the analogy of a rider and an elephant to describe the relationship between intuitive, automatic thinking (elephant) and deliberative, intentional reasoning (rider). The rider observes and comments on what the elephant is doing, but the elephant ultimately decides what direction it takes. "Moral judgment is not a purely cerebral affair in which we weigh concerns about harm, rights, and justice. It's a kind of rapid, automatic process more akin to the judgments animals make as they move through the world, feeling themselves drawn toward or away from various things. Moral judgment is mostly done by the elephant."[3]

This is problematic because people do not even realize they are doing it. They tend to think ethical reasoning comes first and inclinations follow. That is, they tend to think the rider tells the elephant where to go, and the elephant obeys. Here is Haidt again: "Intuitions come first, *strategic* reasoning second. We lie, cheat, and cut ethical corners quite often when we think we can get away with it, and then we use our moral thinking to manage our reputations and justify ourselves to others. We believe our own post hoc reasoning so thoroughly that we end up self-righteously convinced of our own virtue."[4]

The reason this happens is not that people lack reasoning ability but that they are so incredibly skilled at it. The ability to think quickly and easily, to generate multiple reasons, and to express oneself in a convincing fashion, makes it easier to indulge in self-deception regarding one's own conduct.

Albert Bandura, the Stanford psychologist who founded social learning theory, identified eight distinct ways in which

---

3. Jonathan Haidt, *The Righteous Mind: Why Good People Are Divided by Politics and Religion* (New York: Vintage Books, 2012), 72.

4. Ibid., 220.

people commonly subvert moral reasoning to their own advantage in an effort to convince themselves and others that their beliefs or actions are justified or that they are not responsible for some action or failure to act. He calls these "mechanisms of moral disengagement."[5]

1. Moral Justification: excusing bad conduct by suggesting it serves some greater moral purpose. Example: "I lied only because I didn't want to hurt her feelings."

2. Euphemistic Language: using words to make an action seem morally better than it really is. Example: "I didn't actually steal the money; I just borrowed it without his permission."

3. Advantageous Comparison: making one's behavior look better by comparing it to something worse. Example: "There's nothing wrong with cheating a little bit on your taxes. I know one guy who only reports half his income."

4. Displacement of Responsibility: blaming another for one's action or inaction. Example: "I felt then and I still do that I acted as I was directed, and I carried out the orders that I was given, and I do not feel wrong in doing so."[6]

5. Diffusion of Responsibility: minimizing one's own responsibility by drawing attention to similar actions by others. Example: "Everyone was greedy. I just went along."[7]

6. Distortion of Consequences: making it appear that the effects of an action are less significant than they really are. Example: "Well, technically it might be stealing, but it's not like this company will miss a little box of paper clips."

---

5. Albert Bandura, "Selective Moral Disengagement in the Exercise of Moral Agency," *Journal of Moral Education* 31 (2002): 101–19.

6. Lt. William Calley, who was convicted of murdering South Vietnamese civilians in the My Lai Massacre. The transcript of Lt. William Calley's court-martial is available online at *http://law2.umkc.edu/faculty/projects/ftrials/mylai/myl_Calltest.html.*

7. Bernard Madoff, who received a 150-year sentence for defrauding investors, made this remark in an interview from prison. Steve Fishman, "The Madoff Tapes," *New York Magazine*, February 27, 2011, *http://nymag.com/news/features/berniemadoff-2011-3/.*

7. Blaming the Victim: Claiming that the person who was harmed by one's behavior was at fault. Example: "Mr. Jeffreys should not have to pay restitution to individuals who made poor decisions."[8]

8. Dehumanization: Characterizing a person or group of people as less than human in order to justify one's actions. Example: "Anti-Semitism is exactly the same as delousing. Getting rid of lice is not a question of ideology, it is a matter of cleanliness."[9]

One additional way of using moral reasoning for one's own ends is what might be called "partial engagement." It occurs when a person employs some of the four modes of ethical thinking without acknowledging or even suspecting the relevance of the other modes of thinking. Unlike the techniques of moral disengagement, this does not involve subverting the process of moral reasoning; rather, it consists in narrowing one's focus so one only thinks about the way (or ways) of thinking that supports one's position.

To see how this works, consider the following example:

Scott works in the human resources department of a large company. He has had a great deal of training and experience in resolving ethical conflicts. But like many people, he compartmentalizes his work life and his home life. It does not occur to him that the same ethics training he employs at work could be used elsewhere in his life.

One evening, after a particularly tiring day, he comes home from work to find his wife, Corinne, and his thirteen-year-old son, Evan, having a heated discussion in the kitchen. Evan wants to participate in a sleepover at a friend's house along with three other boys his age. Corinne does not think it is a good idea.

During the course of their discussion, Corinne puts forth several reasons for not allowing Evan to participate in the sleepover, all of them focused solely on "consequences":

---

8. Greg Jeffreys, who was ordered by a judge to pay $9.3 million to victims of his real estate scam. Shawn Vestal, "Jeffreys Fraud Case Spreads Plenty of Blame," *Spokesman-Review*, July 11, 2014, *http://www.spokesman.com/stories/2014/jun/11/shawn-vestal-jeffreys-fraud-case-spreads-plenty/*.

9. Heinrich Himmler, "Speech to SS Officers," April 24, 1943, Kharkiv, Ukraine. Reprinted in *US Office of Chief of Counsel for the Prosecution of Axis Criminality, Nazi Conspiracy and Aggression*, 11 vols. (Washington, DC: US Government Printing Office, 1946), 4:572–78, at 574.

- "It's a school night. You have to get up early in the morning."
- "You have a biology test tomorrow. If you don't get enough sleep, you won't do well on the test."
- "You say you'll go to bed early, but you guys will stay up talking half the night without even realizing it. Then you will drag around and be crabby all day."

Evan also puts forth several reasons in support of being allowed to go on the sleepover, all grounded in the idea of "fairness":

- "The other kids can all go on the sleepover. Why can't you treat me like the other parents treat their kids?"
- "I'm old enough to make decisions for myself."
- "When I have kids, I'm not going to treat them like this."

The argument has already been going on for about twenty minutes when Scott walks in the door. Corinne and Evan both turn to him to break the deadlock in their argument. Without having witnessed the prior twenty minutes of conversation, and only picking up on a couple key pieces of information, namely "sleepover" and "school night," he blithely repeats the very same reasons for rejecting Evan's request that Corinne has already expressed. Evan stomps up the stairs in frustration and slams the door to his room, brooding over the misfortune of having parents who will not treat him with the respect and autonomy he deserves. Corinne and Scott remain in the kitchen, commiserating over the challenges of raising a teenage son so deficient in reason and common sense.

The next day when Scott gets to work, he reflects on the previous evening's dispute. He is not so tired now. Fresh and ready to take on the day's challenges, he wonders whether he and Corinne could have handled the situation differently. Why, he wonders, did he start giving his opinion on the matter as soon as he walked in the door? He would never do that with a dispute at work. He would always start by asking questions, making sure everyone is "on the same page." Then he would have followed up with the facts. Why, he wonders, didn't he and Corinne call the parents of the other kids involved in the proposed sleepover? Were they all having the same arguments in their homes? Was the entire dispute even necessary?

What happened in the argument between Evan and his parents is that both sides latched onto the one way of thinking that best supported the position they were already inclined to take. Evan (as children often do) reasoned from "fairness" because that allowed him to argue for greater freedom. Corinne and Scott (as parents often do) reasoned from "consequences" because that allowed them to focus on their goal of ensuring that their children do well in school. Both sides were satisfied that they were in the right, because, after all, they had used ethical reasoning, and, within the narrow confines they had set for themselves, their reasoning was sound. What both parties failed to recognize was that the other side was using ethical reasoning as well, and because of their narrow focus they had not effectively engaged the other's legitimate (albeit limited) ethical concerns.

Whenever people are generating ethical reasons on the intuitive level, even though they may be using those reasons in an attempt to persuade the other to change his or her mind, their reasons are not really guiding the decision making. Rather, the decision making tends to take place first; reasons are then generated to support the decisions. Nevertheless, most people will believe, quite sincerely, that their position is justified and whoever is arguing against them is therefore defending an unjustified position. From there, it is an easy step to conclude that those who oppose one's view are deficient somehow in sincerity or rationality. This is especially evident when parties in a dispute are using different types of ethical reasoning. As long as people who are in a dispute are thinking solely on the intuitive, habitual level, they will be more focused on the fact that they disagree than on the types of reasons they are using to support their respective positions. And if they are using different types of reasons, all their efforts at explanation will be fruitless—words passing through the air without effectively engaging the other side.

All ethical reasoning, whether at work or at home, requires the same habits and skills. One must be willing to listen carefully to what others are saying, engage the situation in a reflective (not a reactive) manner, and thoughtfully consider the different ways of ethical thinking. To do this consistently, it is useful to have a practical method for ethical decision making.

Organizational Hero
HERBERT J. TAYLOR

In 1932, Herbert J. Taylor had a successful career as vice president with the Jewel Tea Company of Chicago, but he put everything at risk when he accepted an invitation to help a struggling company avoid bankruptcy.

The Club Aluminum Company had once been a proud manufacturer of American cookware sold by door-to-door salesmen. But the Great Depression had decimated the company's sales and left it $400,000 in debt. In the beginning, Taylor just served as an advisor to the company, but as he began uncovering the extent of its difficulties, he realized he needed to devote all his energy to its recovery. He left his position at Jewel, accepted an 80 percent cut in pay, and invested $6,100 of his own money in Club Aluminum. Taylor may have been the only one in the company to believe in its products and people, but he had a plan for turning things around. In his autobiography, he recalled those early days:

> The first job was to set policies for the company that would reflect the high ethics and morals God would want in any business. If the people who worked for Club Aluminum were to think right, I knew they would do right. What we needed was a simple, easily remembered guide to right conduct—a sort of ethical yardstick— which all of us in the company could memorize and apply to what we thought, said and did.
>
> I searched through many books for the answer to our need, but the right phrases eluded me, so I did what I often do when I have a problem I can't answer myself: I turn to the One who has all the answers. I leaned over my desk, rested my head in my hands and prayed. After a few moments, I looked up and reached

Continued

Organizational Hero: HERBERT J. TAYLOR *Continued*

for a white paper card. Then I wrote down the twenty-four words that had come to me:

> Is it the truth?
> Is it fair to all concerned?
> Will it build goodwill and better friendships?
> Will it be beneficial to all concerned?
> I called it "The Four-Way Test" of the things we think, say or do.[10]

Creating the Four-Way Test was one thing; implementing it was another. Taylor urged his staff to use the guide at every point of decision making, and it soon came to infuse and even define the company's culture. The marketing department eliminated broad comparative words like "greatest" and "best" from its advertisements, using, instead, factual descriptions of the company's products. Contracts were scrupulously evaluated for honesty and fairness. Here is how author Darrell Thompson describes a particularly difficult decision at the company:

> One day, the sales manager announced a possible order for 50,000 utensils. Sales were low and the company was still struggling at the bankruptcy level. The senior managers certainly needed and wanted that sale, but there was a hitch. The sales manager learned that the potential customer intended to sell the products at cut-rate prices. "That wouldn't be fair to our regular dealers who have been advertising and promoting our product consistently," he said. In one of the toughest decisions the company made that year, the order was turned down. There was no question this transaction would have

Continued

10. Herbert J. Taylor, *The Herbert J. Taylor Story* (Downers Grove, IL: Intervarsity Press, 1968), 40–41. Quoted in "Herbert Taylor," ANBHF Laureates, American National Business Hall of Fame, *http://anbhf.org/laureates/herbert-taylor/*.

> **Organizational Hero:** HERBERT J. TAYLOR *Continued*
>
> made a mockery out of The Four-Way Test the company professed to live by.[11]
>
> Over the course of the next five years, Club Aluminum paid off its debts and began a steady growth in profitability that continued throughout Taylor's tenure with the company.
>
> Rotary International adopted the Four-Way Test in 1943, and today it is used all over the world to inspire ethical business practices.

The Four-Way Method

To avoid the ethical lapses and interpersonal frustrations that arise so frequently in ethically challenging situations, one can employ various strategies for getting people to think more thoroughly and deliberately about what kind of behavior is appropriate in a given situation. Just about any strategy that gets people to step back and take a more critical approach to a situation will have some benefit in this regard, because it will move people from the intuitive to the reflective level of ethical reasoning. But a really effective decision-making method must do more than this. It must also address the problem of moral disengagement by promoting meaningful, critical dialogue that challenges the tendency toward self-deception, and it must address the problem of partial engagement by ensuring the use of all four ways of ethical thinking.

The traditional method of teaching ethics by training students in ethical theories—usually utilitarianism, deontology, and virtue theory—and then practicing the application of the theories to situations in the workplace, has the merit of encouraging students to think at the reflective level, but it does not address the significant dangers of moral disengagement or partial engagement. In fact, such a method exacerbates those dangers, first by introducing complex

---

11. Darrell Thompson, "A Story Behind the Four-Way Test," *A History of the Presidents of Rotary International*, *http://www.rotaryfirst100.org/presidents/1954taylor /taylor/storybehind.htm#.VViQxflVhBd.*

terminology that is often not shared by others with whom one must work through solutions in the case of an ethical crisis[12] and, second, by suggesting that the major ethical theories are mutually exclusive.[13]

The method advanced in this book developed out of an attempt to take advantage of the sophisticated, but intuitive, ethical thinking that most adults already employ on a regular basis while, at the same time, discouraging the tendencies to subvert that reasoning by strategies of moral disengagement or partial engagement. It recognizes that people are already quite familiar with four basic modes of ethical thinking. The aim is to get them to use those four ways of thinking more deliberately, consistently, and thoroughly, and thereby to engage others in constructive dialogue with a chance at attaining consensus or at least making clear the basis for the disagreements.

Whenever somebody thinks about what is right or wrong, good or bad, he or she thinks in terms of one or more of four ways of thinking, described here as *truth, consequences, fairness,* and *character.* Another way to put it is to say that these are the four ways of thinking that have morally persuasive power. If one wants to convince someone that a certain action ought to be done, for example, these ways of thinking provide the sorts of reasons that might legitimately persuade him or her to agree.[14]

---

12. Hannah Arendt discusses Adolf Eichmann's insistence that he was following Kant's ethical principle in carrying out the "final solution"; although her commentary is intended to show how Eichmann misinterpreted Kant's ethics, it also reveals how easily ethical theories can be subverted into serving as rationalization for one's conduct. Hannah Arendt, *Eichmann in Jerusalem* (New York: Penguin, 1963), 135–37.

13. I say that the traditional method of teaching ethics "suggests" that the major theories are mutually exclusive because so many contemporary ethical theorists tend to identify themselves (or be identified by others) as, say, "a utilitarian," or "a Kantian," or "a virtue theorist," and also because the major historical proponents of the theories are often regarded as having believed in the exclusivity of their respective theories. Of course, Aristotle never argued for the exclusivity of one theory, because the other major theories had not yet been advanced. And philosophers like Onora O'Neill have convincingly argued that a proper reading of Kant integrates consequentialism and the virtues into a deontological framework. See Onora O'Neill, *Constructions of Reason: Explorations of Kant's Practical Philosophy* (Cambridge, [England]: Cambridge University Press, 1989).

14. The Four-Way Method presented here is described in much more detail in Richard Kyte, *An Ethical Life: A Practical Guide to Ethical Reasoning* (Winona, MN: Anselm Academic, 2012). The method is influenced by the "Four Topics Method," developed for use in health care settings and described in Albert R. Jonsen, Mark Siegler, and William J. Winslade, *Clinical Ethics,* 5th ed. (New York: McGraw-Hill, 2002).

Four-Way Method for Ethical Decision Making

- What are the facts?
- What are the relevant laws?
- What is the institutional/company policy?
- What are the relevant professional standards?
- What are the possible solutions to the problem?

For each proposed solution:
- Who are those most likely to be affected?
- How are they likely to be affected?
- Which solution will be most beneficial and/or least harmful to those affected?

TRUTH

CONSEQUENCES

CHARACTER

FAIRNESS

- Can the proposed solutions be enacted virtuously (i.e., compassionately, wisely, courageously, etc.)?
- Will doing the proposed actions tend to make the agent(s) more or less virtuous?
- Can the proposed solutions be implemented in a way that builds trusting relationships?

- Do the proposed solutions treat others the way you would want to be treated?
- Do the proposed solutions treat all involved with respect and dignity?
- Are the proposed solutions motivated by goodwill?
- Do the proposed solutions enhance or diminish the autonomy of all involved?

To make thoughtful, deliberate ethical decisions, begin with questions about truth and then proceed through consequences and fairness to character, spending time on each of the four ways of thinking.

Truth

The first of the four ways of ethical thinking is *truth*. It is characterized by the attempt to understand the relevant context of a situation. Determining the truth of a situation does not mean knowing absolutely everything about it but, rather, acquiring a basic understanding of the relevant facts. Because the goal of ethical decision making is right action, truth here is focused on practical knowledge. One interested in the truth might ask questions about what is really happening, what the applicable laws or policies in a given situation might be, and what has happened in the past to shape present conditions or people's perceptions.

Of the four ways of thinking, truth is probably the most essential and the most likely to be overlooked. Because most people do not realize how selective their own perception of events is, they may assume that those who have some basic familiarity with a given situation have an appreciation of the same facts. That assumption is rarely warranted.

Take, for example, the ongoing controversy over the causes of global climate change. Most Americans have access to the same news sources, weather reports, historical data, and scientific studies. And yet Americans are significantly divided on this subject. In a 2013 survey, the Pew Research Center for People and the Press found that 67 percent of Americans think there is "solid evidence that the earth has been getting warmer" while 26 percent think there is "no solid evidence."[15]

This example illustrates why truth is critical when it comes to ethical decision making. Without a shared understanding of the causes underlying climate change, there is little chance that arguments over what to do about it will have any significant persuasive influence. After all, there is little point debating the possible economic consequences of a worldwide carbon tax with people who do not think the release of carbon into the atmosphere affects the climate.

Socrates argued that the greatest threat to ethics is ignorance: thinking one knows what one does not know.[16] Therefore, the first step toward being ethical is to counter one's tendency toward self-deception by opening up one's beliefs to public scrutiny. In the give-and-take of open discussion, it becomes harder to convince oneself that one's understanding of things is sufficient.

Consequences

Thinking in terms of *consequences* (i.e., results, effects, and pros and cons) is the most widely used way of ethical thinking in American society.[17] Most public policy decisions, for example, are defended

---

15. *http://www.people-press.org/2013/11/01/gop-deeply-divided-over-climate-change*.

16. Plato, *Apology*, in *The Trial and Death of Socrates*, trans. G.M.A. Grube, rev. C.D.C. Reeve (Indianapolis: Hackett, 1975), 21d.

17. In many societies around the world, especially those characterized by adherence to local customs and traditions, *character* is the preferred mode of thinking about ethical matters.

primarily on the basis of the effects likely to result from a given policy. Employees are often evaluated primarily based on the results of their efforts. Terms such as "bottom line," "cost-benefit analysis," and "outcome-based assessment" are pervasive in organizational speech.

And yet there is little consistency regarding the use of consequences to influence conduct. To think about consequences from an ethical perspective, one must take into account the many ways in which potential actions could affect those involved. This can be done by asking the following questions:

1. What are the possible options (or courses of action) available?
2. Who is affected by each option?
3. How are they affected (positively or negatively and to what extent)?
4. Which option has the greatest overall positive effect or the least overall negative effect?

It is important to make these questions explicit and to consider each of them carefully, because the natural tendency is to think of the consequences affecting oneself first and to give them more weight than they deserve. By making the questions explicit, one is forced to pay attention to the consequences for all, regardless of one's relation to or interest in them.

The theory corresponding to this way of thinking is utilitarianism. It was first proposed in the eighteenth century by Jeremy Bentham, an English philosopher and political reformer.[18]

Fairness

The easiest way to think about fairness is to recall the Golden Rule: "Always treat others the way you would like to be treated." The Golden Rule does not function as a detailed guide to behavior but, rather, as a reminder to imagine a situation from the other's point of view before doing something that affects him or her. As such, it expresses a commitment to equality: if you and I

---

18. Jeremy Bentham, *The Principles of Morals and Legislation* (Amherst, NY: Prometheus Books, 1988).

are morally equal, then your perspective and my perspective are equally significant when it comes to determining how I should act. In this way, one is discouraged from privileging one's own perspective or interests.[19]

Another way of thinking about fairness is in terms of respect. To treat someone with respect is to treat them as if they really matter, as someone who has inherent worth and dignity. Being polite or courteous are signs of respect, but of course it goes much deeper than that. It means granting to others the same rights and privileges one demands for oneself.

Generally speaking, fairness focuses more on process or procedure than on outcomes. The rules for the game of Monopoly are fair because they treat everyone the same. Everybody starts with the same amount of money, from the same position on the board, and has the same opportunities for buying and selling property. But the rules do not ensure that everyone ends up with the same results.

Many people find the concept of fairness difficult to grasp, most likely because the word is sometimes used to express one's feelings about some outcome or other. For example, a person might say, "The lottery is fair to the winners but not to the losers." But that would be a misuse of the term. All the speaker really means is something like: "The winners like the outcome of the lottery and the losers do not." But fairness has nothing to do with whether one likes the outcome. It only has to do with whether people were treated equally and with respect. If a lottery is conducted honestly, provides all participants with the same odds of winning, and is voluntary, then it is fair.

Consider this example: Two children, Anna and Anton, are given a piece of licorice to share. Anna starts to cut the piece in two, but Anton, suspecting that she is about to cut a bigger piece for herself, objects. "Wait a minute," he says. "If you cut the licorice, then I get to choose my piece first. Or I could cut the licorice, and you can choose first." Anna considers this, then agrees. She cuts the licorice,

---

19. Some have proposed the so-called Platinum Rule as an improvement on the Golden Rule: "Always treat others as *they* would like to be treated." But actually, it is the same rule, just expressed differently. The point is to fully consider the other's point of view and to make that the basis of one's action. Another way to put it would be to say something like, "Always treat others the way you would want to be treated *if you saw things from their perspective.*"

making sure that both halves are just the same length. Notice in this example that the procedure would be fair even if Anna did not cut the licorice precisely in half. As long as they both understand and agree to the procedure, it is fair. The actual outcome—and how each party feels about the outcome—is irrelevant.

Immanuel Kant has provided the most comprehensive account of ethical reasoning on the basis of fairness. He claimed that ethical obligation can be reduced to a single principle, the Categorical Imperative: "Always act in the way that you would want anyone else in the same situation to have to act."[20] The Categorical Imperative is similar to the Golden Rule but much broader in scope. Whereas the Golden Rule asks one to engage in reversibility ("putting one-self in another's shoes"), the Categorical Imperative asks one to engage in universalizability, by considering what would happen if everyone acted in a certain way, with the same intention. Kant thought that this would rule out certain broad categories of behavior, notably lying, manipulation, and coercion, making them always morally impermissible.

Character

To think in terms of character is to evaluate actions in light of the character traits that produce them. For example, to consider whether giving a gift would be a good thing to do, one would ask if the gift-giving would be an expression of generosity (as opposed to asking how one would feel if one were the recipient of the gift, or what the costs and benefits might be). If the gift-giving is motivated by a desire to influence a sale and not by generosity, then the act might be morally questionable. In short, the focus of character thinking is primarily on the person—specifically the motivation of the person—and only secondarily on the action the person performs.

---

20. See Immanuel Kant, *Grounding for the Metaphysics of Morals*, trans. James W. Ellington, 3rd ed. (Indianapolis: Hackett, 1993), 30. Actually, Kant puts it this way: "Act as if the maxim of your action were to become by your will a universal law of nature." I have simplified the Categorical Imperative here because the purpose of this section of the book is to point out the way in which Kant's ethical theory grounds and extends the idea of fairness as the foundation of ethics, not to engage in an in-depth discussion of Kant's theory.

Character traits generally fall into two broad categories: virtues and vices. Virtues are traits that tend to lead to happiness (i.e., well-being or fulfillment); vices are traits that tend to lead to unhappiness. Because happiness and unhappiness are so intimately entwined with the quality of people's relationships, many virtues turn out to be those traits that enhance healthy relationships with others and the corresponding vices turn out to be the traits that undermine healthy relationships. Honesty, for example, is a virtue because it is the foundation of trust, and trust is essential for relationships of mutual respect and friendship. Dishonesty is a vice because it destroys trust, thereby damaging the quality of one's relationships with others. At the end of life, people who have been consistently dishonest are much more likely to find themselves isolated and dissatisfied.

The most influential account of ethical thinking according to character comes from Aristotle in the *Nicomachean Ethics*. In that work, he argues that happiness is the ultimate goal that everyone seeks and that virtues, such as courage, generosity, justice, temperance, and wisdom, are the keys to happiness.[21] They do not guarantee that a person will be happy, but genuine happiness cannot be attained without them.

Organizational Hero
DAVE SKOGEN

Dave's career in the grocery business began when he was just four years old. His parents, Paul and Jane Skogen, bought a neighborhood grocery store in 1946, and they moved with their family into the house attached to the store. Dave and his brothers worked in the store after school and on weekends, sorting pop bottles and packaging goods. After graduating from high school,

Continued

---

21. The word Aristotle uses for the ultimate goal is *eudaimonia*, which is often translated as "happiness" but carries a richer meaning than that word typically conveys. A more apt translation would be something like "flourishing" or "fulfillment." See Aristotle, *Nicomachean Ethics*, trans. C.D.C. Reeve (Indianapolis: Hackett, 2014).

Organizational Hero: Dave Skogen *Continued*

Dave worked full-time at the meat counter, butchering chickens and turkeys alongside his Grandpa Orris. Eventually, Dave took over the family business and began to expand, growing the operation to what is today more than twenty large Festival Foods supermarkets employing more than five thousand full- and part-time associates.

Transitioning from the neighborhood grocery store to a chain of supermarkets meant competing head-to-head with major retailers like Walmart and Cub Foods, and that required not just learning new ways to sell groceries but new and better ways to create a culture where employees would thrive and to which customers would want to return. Dave calls this the "boomerang theory." He writes,

> Behind boomeranging is the idea that extraordinary hospitality rather than ordinary service brings people back. It means going that extra mile for your customers, who will then go the extra mile to come back to your business.
>
> It also includes the belief that we need to care about our associates, because they will provide better customer service when they are satisfied with their work.

When it comes to improving the culture at Festival Foods, Dave is relentless. No opportunity for improvement is overlooked, and that means everything from making sure aisles are clean, shelves are stocked, and produce is fresh, to providing smiling service and going out of one's way to make another person's day a little bit better.

Creating a boomerang culture wasn't easy. It required getting everybody to buy into servant leadership, starting with Dave himself. One day, Dave asked his leadership team to participate in a 360-degree feedback tool, in which each member solicited evaluations from ten people at various levels within the company.

Continued

Organizational Hero: DAVE SKOGEN *Continued*

When Dave's results came back, he was shocked: he scored low in "listening." That evening, at home, he confided to his wife, Barb. "My associates tell me I'm not a good listener," he said. She replied, "I've been telling you that for years."

Dave was always encouraging people to improve, or, as he puts it, to work on their "stuff." Now his associates were telling him about his "stuff," and he needed to do something about it. So he took all his white shirts and had the cuffs embroidered with the words "Listen first." Dave put his "stuff" out in public for customers and associates to see. He says, "It helped me remain aware of what I needed to work on day after day."

Dave understands that if he wants to have a positive influence on others, he has to start with himself. Even today, at more than seventy years old, he is still working on that. As he likes to say, "I'm not as good as I want to be, but I am better than I used to be."[22]

Decision Making in Practice

The Four-Way Method does not guarantee that one will reach the correct decision in every case, nor does it provide a sure way of resolving conflicts, either in one's own thinking or among a group of people. Sometimes this process may bring conflicting considerations to light that may otherwise have remained obscured. It may even cause one to be less confident about one's decisions, but that is not always a bad thing. What the Four-Way Method can do is ensure that the process of decision making is clearer and more thorough by forcing one to pay attention not just to *what* one is thinking about but to *how* one is thinking about it. And it can help do this in a number of different ways.

---

22. Dave Skogen, *Boomerang! Leadership Principles That Bring the Customer Back* (Green Bay, WI: Ninth Street, 2013).

The first way of using the Four-Way Method is as a tool for self-reflection, helping one to step back and consider a situation carefully and deliberately. It is human nature to jump to conclusions first and then generate reasons afterwards, but if one takes time to think carefully, using each way of thinking in turn, one is less likely to commit to a decision that seems intuitively plausible only because it satisfies one's interests. Sometimes, thinking through each of the four ways of ethical reasoning allows one to find additional, mutually supportive reasons to support a decision. Sometimes, it may reveal that there are conflicting reasons of which one was not previously aware. One might discover, for example, that a proposal one has been working on to restructure the company and that would benefit the majority of employees, would also be unfair to some of the people affected. The Four-Way Method would not necessarily show how to resolve the conflict, but by bringing the conflict to light, it would allow one to go back to the drawing board, to see whether there might be a way of improving the plan without being unfair to some employees. Or, knowing about the conflict might change how one plans to announce the plan for restructuring. This brings us to another way of using the Four-Way Method.

Leaders in organizations frequently find themselves faced with having to communicate controversial decisions to others who, for one reason or another, have not been part of the decision-making process. For example, in the case of a significant restructuring plan, leaders in the organization may want to include, in the announcement, some reference to all four ways of thinking, otherwise the strongest objections may come from the ways of thinking they do not address. They might want to address *truth* by making sure that all the relevant information about the restructuring is conveyed, paying particular attention to the sorts of things that might be easily misunderstood or have already become the subject of rumors. They might want to address *consequences* of various options by noting the likely positive and negative effects for everyone affected by the restructuring. They might want to talk about *fairness* by emphasizing the process whereby the plan was developed and who had input into the decision, paying particular attention to the ways in which the voices of various stakeholders were either acknowledged or neglected. Finally, they might want to address *character* by saying something about the motivation for the plan, in an effort to assure people of their desire to maintain trust and goodwill. Communicating in this way does not ensure there will be no misunderstandings or disagreements. After all, when significant changes take place in an organization, people's interests are affected in different ways, and those interests do not go away because of a good communication strategy. However, one can try to ensure that disagreements remain honest, that is, not based on misunderstanding or deception.

Using the Four-Way Method to communicate potentially controversial decisions is also important because it encourages one to focus on rational persuasion as a means of influencing others and thus makes it less likely that one will resort to coercive power to get others to go along with a decision.

The third, and most significant, way in which the Four-Way Method may be used is to facilitate joint decision making. Generally, in joint decision making (that is, any decision involving two or more people), one of two things happens: either a dominant person (or group of people) takes over the discussion, or else input is shared by multiple people using different ways of thinking at the same time. In the first situation, attention gets restricted to the dominant person's preferred way of thinking and the quieter people in the group do not get an opportunity to share their insights. In the second situation, the attention of the group continually shifts back and forth from one way of thinking to another. Many possibilities are considered, many reasons are given, but little progress is made toward reaching consensus on what to do.

These sorts of difficulties can be avoided by having a facilitator lead a group in an orderly discussion utilizing each of the four ways of thinking in turn. This ensures all people in the group have an opportunity to express the reasons they find most persuasive and that others in the group will attend to those reasons. If during a discussion of the consequences of a situation, one member raises concerns about fairness, the facilitator can gently remind that member to wait until the group is ready to discuss fairness. In this way even dominant personalities have to wait their turn to weigh in on the discussion, and the more introverted members of the group are encouraged to participate. Also, over the course of the discussion, the members of the group will engage in constructive dialogue because, at each point, each member will be using the same kind of reasoning as the other members.

Again, using this method will not ensure that by the end of the process all parties will agree with one another, but it is a method that at least provides a genuine opportunity for reaching consensus because it greatly diminishes the possibility of sabotage by one of the two great enemies of ethical reasoning: moral disengagement and partial engagement. If at the end of the process people still do not agree on what should be done, it is very likely that at least they will understand *why* there is disagreement, and they should be able to see that the disagreement is reasonable.

One of the aims of a decision-making process is to ensure that even when agreement cannot be reached, the participants have respect for one another as moral agents. If participants end the process by saying something like, "Well, I don't agree, but I understand," that result is much better than participants who depart angrily, thinking to themselves, "I just don't get where they're coming from; could they really not see the right thing to do, or were they just being stubborn?"

Conclusion

As Mark considered how to respond to Robert's report, he glanced at the Four-Way Method diagram lying on his desk. He had been introduced to the method just two weeks before. Now, he thought, would be an opportunity to try it out.

"Robert," he said, "I want to thank you for your quick response to the falling light fixture and your thoroughness in inspecting the other fixtures in the immediate area. But I just want to make sure that we think about this carefully before we make a decision regarding what follow-up actions need to be taken, if any. Here is a decision-making method I learned in a class recently. Do you mind taking a few minutes to go through these questions together? I just want to make sure we have considered everything."

Robert and Mark spent the next twenty minutes going through the Four-Way Method together, answering the questions in turn, raising new questions, occasionally stopping to reflect a bit more thoroughly in some sections, until they came to the end. At that point Robert observed, "I think we need to inspect all the ceiling fixtures." Mark agreed. What really convinced both of them was the discussion they had in the section on fairness. Mark had asked, "What about the employees whose workstations are located underneath lights that have not been inspected?" They both agreed that if they themselves worked at those stations, they would want the lights inspected.

Robert conveyed the discussion he had had with Mark to his crew, and they set about inspecting all the fixtures in the plant. At the end of the week, he reported back to Mark: "We found ten more fixtures with loose bolts. You never know, but we just may have saved a life."

Making an ethical decision for the common good is a matter of finding the right thing to do—in the right way. The "right way," in most cases, is the way that constructively engages others in forming the decision, so that relationships are built and maintained on a foundation of trust.

Discussion Questions

1. How many times a day do you engage in ethical reasoning? Describe an instance when you used ethical reasoning in the past twenty-four hours.

2. Go to the opinion section of a newspaper and read the "Letters to the Editor." Can you identify the ways of ethical thinking used by the letter writers?

3. Of the four ways of ethical thinking, which one is easiest to use? Which one is the most challenging?

4. If you are facilitating a group that is trying to resolve an ethical problem, what is more important, finding the right answer or getting consensus among members of the group?

Resources for Further Exploration

PRINT

Kahneman, Daniel. *Thinking Fast and Slow*. New York: Farrar, Straus and Giroux, 2011.

This fascinating book culminates decades of research conducted by Kahneman and Amos Tversky into the nature, and especially the limitations, of human rationality.

Kyte, Richard. *An Ethical Life: A Practical Guide to Ethical Reasoning.* Winona, MN: Anselm Academic, 2012.

> The Four-Way Method is explained in more detail in this book. Those interested in exploring how the four ways of thinking—truth, consequences, fairness, and character—are related to the major ethical theories are advised to look here.

OTHER MEDIA

Sandel, Michael. "Justice." *http://www.justiceharvard.org/.*

> In his course on justice, this Harvard philosophy professor eloquently demonstrates the relevance of ethical decision making for public deliberation as he discusses classic ethical dilemmas with his students, drawing out the conflicting motivational pulls of utilitarianism, deontology, and virtue theory.

5 CHAPTER

Exercising the Moral Imagination

The most underappreciated trait in ethical decision making is moral imagination: the ability to look at a situation and think of creative ways of responding that effectively redress wrongs, avoid harm, enhance the common good, or set the stage for future ethical conduct. Situations rarely arrive at one's doorstep with all available options identified, described, and ready for selection. Moreover, when one is in the midst of an ongoing situation and events are still unfolding, how one acts initially will influence the ways other events unfold. The person called upon to make a decision is rarely a dispassionate observer, watching events take place as if from a mountaintop. She is more likely to be down in the valley, in the middle of the action, struggling to comprehend what is happening, figuring out what to do as she goes, with only a partial view of the context, and always having to reassess the situation as events take place.

That is why case studies are such an important tool for the student of business ethics. Case studies allow one to examine the particular circumstances of situations calling for an ethical response, imaginatively inhabiting the perspective of the person responsible for making a decision—asking, "What would I do in this situation?"— while also stepping outside the situation, to evaluate as if from high above, taking advantage of a perspective generally not available to the actual participants. Case studies allow one to exercise the moral imagination so that one is ready to act when the time comes.

The ability to switch perspectives is a key part of moral agency, the ability not only to respond to situations but to reflect on those responses and also to reflect on *possible* responses, actions that one considers but does not actually perform. This ability can be studied, practiced, and refined. Ronald Heifetz considers the ability to switch perspectives to be fundamental to good leadership, referring to it as moving off the "dance floor" and getting onto the "balcony."[1]

To exercise the reader's moral imagination, this chapter will examine three case studies: one actual and two fictionalized accounts of real situations. These case studies invite the reader to move back and forth—from a participant's perspective to that of a distanced observer—looking closely at particular details and then stepping back to consider the broader context of the case. Each case represents a different type of ethical problem: a difficult situation faced by an inexperienced employee, a public dispute between a well-known company and its customers, and a difficulty with interpreting an organization's ethics policy. In each case, the Four-Way Method will be employed, using different ways of thinking to exercise the moral imagination and determine the best course of action.

Case Study 1:
The Would-Be Whistle-blower

Michael looked down at his hands, trembling after the close call. The watch on his wrist read 9:07 am. Just seconds before, the upper assembly of the drill press collapsed, nearly smashing his hands. He took a deep breath and looked around the room. The other employees had their heads down, focusing on their work. Didn't they hear the crash? Weren't they curious about what had just happened? Then it struck him; this wasn't an accident. His drill press had been sabotaged. One of his coworkers must have loosened the bolts so that it would collapse as soon as he started using it that morning. Michael turned, walked through the plant, past his coworkers, and out the door. He never returned.

---

1. See Sharon Daloz Parks, *Leadership Can Be Taught: A Bold Approach for a Complex World* (Boston: Harvard Business Review Press, 2005), and Ronald Heifetz, Alexander Grashow, and Marty Linsky, *The Practice of Adaptive Leadership* (Boston: Harvard Business Press, 2009).

Michael's trouble on the job had started just two weeks before. He began experiencing headaches in the afternoons and wondered if they were related to his work. He operated a drill press at a small manufacturing firm that made aftermarket parts for automobiles. About ten feet from his workstation was a vat containing a solvent used to degrease parts prior to assembly. When he finished his drilling process, he would take a tray of parts and place them in the solvent. A strong odor came from the vat, and Michael suspected his headaches were caused by exposure to the unventilated fumes. He asked Ken, his supervisor, what was in the solution. Ken waved him off. "Don't worry about it," he said. "It's just a standard degreaser."

The answer did not satisfy Michael, who happened to be a chemistry major about to begin his junior year at a local university. The next day, when nobody was looking, he slipped a test tube out of his pocket, dipped it into the solution, and sneaked a sample out of the building. He brought it to one of his chemistry professors for analysis. They discovered that the main compound in the solution was methylene chloride, a substance that can cause headaches and nausea from short-term exposure but may also have more serious health effects, such as cancer, heart or liver damage, or injury to the central nervous system, if exposure at high levels occurs over a long period of time.

The following morning, Michael went to see Dave Robinson, the company's owner, whose office was located in the corner of the plant. He told Robinson about his headaches, described how the supervisor had dismissed his concerns and how he then took a sample of the solvent from the facility to have it tested. Finally, he produced the test results, placing them on Robinson's desk with a half dozen informational sheets from the Occupational Safety and Health Administration (OSHA) listing the potential dangers of exposure to methylene chloride along with guidelines for air quality testing and requirements for protecting workers. He paused and looked at Robinson. He wasn't sure what to expect. A little resistance maybe, some questions, perhaps gratitude for showing initiative and concern for his fellow workers. But Robinson just sat there, silent, glowering at the test results.

Then Robinson stood up, leaned forward, and placed one finger firmly in the center of Michael's chest. His voice was low and fierce: "I don't know who you think you are, but I don't need a college student walking into my office, waving a bunch of papers at me, and telling me how to run my business. If you have a problem, you take it up with Ken. Now, get back to work, or get out of my building."

Michael was stunned, embarrassed, angry. He turned around and walked quickly to his workstation. His mind was racing. This was intolerable. Maybe he could live with headaches for the next couple of months, but what about the other employees who worked here year after year? They could be seriously harmed by inhaling the vapors, and neither the owner nor the supervisor cared about that. He couldn't believe their indifference.

During his lunch break, Michael sat down next to a couple of employees who worked on his side of the building. He told them the whole story. They seemed amused by it, but Michael was persistent. "This is a serious issue," he said. "If they aren't going to install a ventilating hood over that solution and provide proper safety training, I'm going to report them to OSHA. They'll come in and shut this place down!" Michael was getting really worked up now.

The accident happened two days later. And even though he never went back to that place, he still thinks about it every day, reliving the chain of events, wondering what he did wrong, what he could have done differently.

The Four-Way Method: Truth

The first step in the Four-Way Method is to consider the truth of the situation, that is, to look at the facts, the overall context, and to identify the possible courses of action that could be taken to resolve the problem.

What were Michael's options once he discovered the presence of methylene chloride in the solution? The first option would be the course he actually did take: report the situation to his superiors and demand changes. That course did not turn out well in this instance, but it did not necessarily have to turn out that way. Another option would be to do nothing. He could wait to see if the headaches went away as he became more accustomed to the conditions and, in the meantime, begin looking for a different job. A third option would be to quietly get more information about the situation, to find out, for example, whether other employees had experienced similar symptoms and whether the company had tested exposure levels. He could do this while also seeking advice about how to proceed from a coworker within the company or a trusted advisor outside the company.

There are two significant problems with the first option (reporting the situation). The first is that Michael proceeded without the advantage of a full understanding of the context of the situation within the company.

Although Michael took an important first step by discovering the presence of methylene chloride in the solution, he did not make a similar effort to discover what his coworkers might already know about the solution, whether they were experiencing headaches, or even whether exposure levels had been measured in the building and whether those levels were within requirements. In considering the truth of a situation, one must not only have a grasp of a few central facts, one must also understand the context of those facts, that is, how they fit into the overall situation.

New employees, especially young people early in their careers, are rarely in a position to correct persistent, intentional wrongdoing in an organization. Even if they have taken an ethics class and can successfully identify and analyze misconduct, they are not thereby granted power to make significant changes. It is more likely, if they stick around long enough, that the organization will gradually change their own attitudes and behavior.

Michael was no exception. He had just taken a business ethics class at his university the previous spring. He could provide a thorough explanation of what was wrong and what should be done about it. But what (in general) should be done about a problem and what Michael (in particular) should do about it were two very different things. Solving this particular problem required someone with authority, and that is precisely what Michael lacked. Nothing in his ethics training helped him understand how to approach a difficult situation like this one, especially how to talk to a supervisor about a sensitive topic or how to talk to his coworkers about it.

The second problem with reporting the situation was even more significant: It failed to anticipate how others were likely to respond to the action. Michael made demands without taking into account his lack of standing with the owner, supervisor, or coworkers. That indicated a serious error in judgment about the context in which he found himself.

The second option (doing nothing) would not require anything at all from Michael, except perhaps to ignore the evidence before him. To do nothing would be to disregard the evidence of the dangers of methylene chloride exposure.

The third option (gathering additional information and seeking advice) would require patience and careful consideration about how to proceed. Michael could have made some general inquiries about safety training. Without accusing anybody of wrongdoing, he could have asked his supervisor if there were any precautions he needed to take around the solution. He could have asked his coworkers about how often they received safety training—an appropriate question from someone who is new to the company and curious about how things are done. He could have mentioned his headaches over lunch to see whether anybody else was experiencing similar symptoms. In such a way, he could have gained a better picture of the overall context of the situation. In addition, Michael needed to find someone in whom to confide. Was there someone within the company he could have talked to about the problem confidentially, someone who could have given him advice about how to proceed? Perhaps there was a coworker who had been with the company a long time and was widely respected, someone who could have brought the information about methylene chloride to the owner in a way that would get him to pay attention. Michael might have found out that the owner really did care about worker safety, or he might have found out that methylene chloride exposure was just one of many serious safety concerns in the plant. If the latter is the case, he would probably want to seek some legal advice about whistle-blowing. How should he proceed? What should he expect? Are there state or federal laws that would provide him with legal protections if he reported violations? It would have been prudent to have such information before going to the owner with a complaint.

The Four-Way Method: Consequences

The first question to consider when thinking about consequences is, who is likely to be significantly affected by one's actions? In Michael's case, there are only a few: himself, his coworkers, and the owner of the company.

In the case of the first option—reporting the situation to his superiors and demanding changes—he has the advantage of looking back and observing what the actual outcome was. And even though Michael intended to have a positive effect on the working environment within the plant, because he did not have the standing to bring his concerns to the owner and supervisor, or even to his coworkers, in a credible and convincing fashion, the outcome was that no actions were taken to address the problem of methylene chloride exposure. Whatever the effects of long-term exposure to methylene chloride might be to his coworkers, the consequence of Michael's action was the same as if he had done nothing at all.

The consequences to Michael, however, were worse than if he had done nothing at all, and they could potentially have been much worse if his hands had been injured by the collapsing drill press.

The second option—to do nothing and look for a different job—would, like the first option, have no considerable effect on the owner and would leave his coworkers with continued exposure to methylene chloride, but it also would have the considerable advantage of being safer for Michael and allowing him to continue earning a wage until he found a new job.

The significant consequence that stands out in both the first and second options is the continued long-term exposure of Michael's coworkers to methylene chloride. How significant is that? It is impossible to know without more information, chiefly, measurements of the levels of exposure and length of time to which various workers had been exposed already. The effects of short-term exposure are reversible, but the seriousness of long-term effects are still unknown. Here is a summary of the risks from the Environmental Protection Agency:

> The acute (short-term) effects of methylene chloride inhalation in humans consist mainly of nervous system effects including decreased visual, auditory, and motor functions, but these effects are reversible once exposure ceases. The effects of chronic (long-term) exposure to methylene chloride suggest that the central nervous system (CNS) is a potential target in humans and animals. Human data are inconclusive regarding methylene chloride and cancer.

Animal studies have shown increases in liver and lung cancer and benign mammary gland tumors following the inhalation of methylene chloride.[2]

The third option is the most promising from the point of view of consequences. Although taking time to gather more information and get advice on how to approach the owner about the situation does not ensure any meaningful changes will take place in the plant, it at least opens up that possibility. It also has the advantage of minimizing the risk of retaliation by coworkers. Would addressing safety concerns at the plant be a negative consequence for the owner? Perhaps. But while there certainly would be some initial financial costs associated with increased safety training and improved ventilation at the plant, the long-term costs are harder to calculate. Improved safety conditions are likely to result in long-term savings from better employee health, fewer sick days, lower insurance premiums, fewer workers' compensation claims, and perhaps even the avoidance of lawsuits.

The Four-Way Method: Fairness

Did Michael act fairly toward the owner of the company? It is tempting to say, "Yes, of course," because Michael did nothing deceptive, manipulative, or coercive. He candidly presented the owner with the information he had discovered about the effects of methylene chloride exposure and the relevant safety requirements. But in considering fairness, one must consider not only *what* is done but *how* it is done. Was Michael's approach to the owner respectful? If Michael could imagine himself in the owner's role, is that the way he would want to be approached? These questions are posed not to excuse the owner's conduct, but merely to point out that the owner's dismissal of Michael's legitimate concerns may have been prompted not by disregard for worker safety but by indignation at Michael's manner. And while the owner certainly deserves to know about the exposure

---

2. "Methylene Chloride (Dichloromethane): Hazard Summary—Created in April 1992; Revised in January 2000," US Environmental Protection Agency, *http://www.epa.gov/ttnatw01/hlthef/methylen.html*.

dangers, he should be presented with the information in an appropriate manner. What would be appropriate in this case? That is where the third option comes into play. A person who knew more about the owner, especially whether he had a history of disregard or concern for worker safety, could have helped Michael figure out the best way to approach his boss with the information.

What about fairness toward his coworkers? Michael had a responsibility to inform them about the potential dangers and, perhaps, even take action by reporting the violations to OSHA. Even though one or more of them retaliated against Michael by sabotaging the drill press, that didn't absolve him of responsibility to the others. And what about future workers, including the person who ends up replacing Michael? How would he want others to act if they were in his situation? For that matter, wouldn't Michael have wished that someone who had been working there longer, perhaps someone who also had experienced headaches and wondered about the cause, had investigated and brought this issue out into the open? And if he wished that, didn't he have the responsibility to do just what he wished others had already done?

Michael must also face the fact that even though he did not intend it, he acted in a way that one or more of his coworkers most likely regarded as arrogant. To come into a temporary job and talk seriously about taking actions that could threaten the livelihood of long-term employees could certainly be seen as disrespectful. It is not disrespectful to care about safety, but Michael expressed that concern by assuming he knew what was in the best interest of everyone else in the plant. He did not trust the autonomy of his coworkers, that is, their ability and their right to understand and make decisions about their own working conditions.

Without knowing more about the personalities involved in this case and the general attitude taken toward safety issues in the plant, it is difficult to know whether there is any approach Michael could have taken that would have been effective in preventing harm, but one can assess whether certain approaches take into account the moral capacities of the owner and the coworkers. That is why, from the point of view of fairness, Michael should have selected the third option: take time to gather relevant information and seek advice about how to proceed from someone more experienced.

The Four-Way Method: Character

An important thing for any employee to think about is how to build trusting relationships within the company so that the employee understands the motivations of others and that those others, in turn, understand the employee's motivations. Building trust requires time. It grows slowly as a result of mutual, consistent experiences of good character. And time is precisely what Michael did not have.

Did Michael have courage? He certainly seemed to, since he did not hesitate to sneak a sample of the solvent from the plant and then to confront the owner of the company with the results of the chemical analysis. But was this really courage, or rashness? Michael didn't exactly face down the dangers confronting him; rather, he seemed unaware of them. He was surprised that the owner was angry with him for bringing attention to the safety violations, and he was completely unprepared for retaliation from a coworker. To put oneself in danger out of ignorance, even with the best of intentions, is not courageous. It is foolish.

Nor do Michael's actions reveal practical wisdom. Michael pursued the shortest course at each turn, doing what promised the quickest solution to the problem, without considering whether the shortest course was the most effective. Perhaps the virtue Michael needed most was patience. He needed to take time to think about what to do. And because he was new to the company and inexperienced, he needed to seek advice. He needed to compensate for his own lack of wisdom with the wisdom of someone who had more experience in situations like this one, more understanding of how organizations work, and, significantly, knowledge of how to talk effectively to people about contentious issues.

Summary

Using all four ways of ethical thinking, and considering the three likely options available to Michael in light of them, it is clear that he needed to choose the third option. By gathering more information and seeking advice from someone else, preferably a coworker who had been with the company for a while and who is trusted by others, Michael could then have formulated a plan of action with the best overall consequences, being respectful of others' autonomy and embodying the virtues of courage and wisdom. There is no guarantee, of course, that acting in that way will result in changes to safety conditions at the plant, but it offers the best hope of such a result.

Case Study 2:
Netflix and Ethics of Apology

When Reed Hastings and Marc Randolph founded Netflix in 1997, they could not have anticipated how quickly the company would grow and how much the industry would change over the next eighteen years. Starting out as a subscription service for DVD rentals by mail, they had 4.2 million members by 2005.[3] Their growth was based on convenience, low price, and a reputation for excellent customer service.

In 2007, Netflix introduced online streaming, giving its members the option to watch programs instantly on their computers rather than waiting for DVDs to arrive in the mailbox. Streaming proved popular and cost-effective, and Netflix's early adoption of the technology allowed the company to greatly expand its customer base. Today, it has more than fifty-seven million members in nearly fifty countries around the world.[4] But the rapid growth and transformation of the company into a global media provider did not come without significant miscues that led to public questioning of the company's integrity.

From the beginning, one of Netflix's challenges has been creating customer loyalty when customers have virtually no direct interaction with employees. Hastings focused on the indirect approach: create a great internal culture and expect that to translate into a positive customer experience. "We want our employees to have great freedom—freedom to be brilliant or freedom to make mistakes," said Hastings. And so they developed innovative policies, like unlimited vacation time and flexibility in how pay and benefits are structured.[5]

---

3. Netflix Media Center, *https://pr.netflix.com/WebClient/loginPageSalesNetWorks Action.do?contentGroupId=10477*.

4. "Company Profile," Netflix, *http://ir.netflix.com/*.

5. Ryan Blitstein, "Work Zone: A Bottomless Well of Vacation Time," *Pittsburgh Post-Gazette*, April 2, 2007, *http://www.post-gazette.com/businessnews/2007/04/02/Work -Zone-A-bottomless-well-of-vacation-time/stories/200704020127#ixzz0SWCX0I9B*.

That strategy paid off with some of the highest customer satisfaction rankings in the nation. For six consecutive years, from 2005 through 2010, Netflix had the top scores in the Foresee Experience Index for Web retailers.[6] But in 2011, Netflix announced two big changes: a price increase of $6 per month and dividing the streaming and DVD services into separate operations. The DVD service would have a new name: Qwikster. The negative reaction from customers was immediate and severe. In the next few weeks, they lost 800,000 customers. CEO Reed Hastings issued a public apology:

> I messed up. I owe everyone an explanation.
>
> It is clear from the feedback over the past two months that many members felt we lacked respect and humility in the way we announced the separation of DVD and streaming, and the price changes. That was certainly not our intent, and I offer my sincere apology. I'll try to explain how this happened. . . .
>
> When Netflix is evolving rapidly, however, I need to be extra-communicative. This is the key thing I got wrong.
>
> In hindsight, I slid into arrogance based upon past success. We have done very well for a long time by steadily improving our service, without doing much CEO communication. Inside Netflix I say, "Actions speak louder than words," and we should just keep improving our service.
>
> But now I see that given the huge changes we have been recently making, I should have personally given a full justification to our members of why we are separating DVD and streaming, and charging for both. It wouldn't have changed the price increase, but it would have been the right thing to do.[7]

Hastings' apology was remarkable for its candor, but while it earned praise from some analysts[8] and the company continued to grow once the controversy died down, the former high levels of

6. "The Foresee Experience Index (FXI): 2013 US Retail Edition," *http://www.foresee.com/assets/foresee-fxi-us-retail-edition-2013.pdf.*

7. Reed Hastings, "An Explanation and Some Reflections," Netflix, September 18, 2011, *http://blog.netflix.com/2011/09/explanation-and-some-reflections.html.*

8. See Andrew Ross Sorkin, "Too Many Sorry Excuses for Apology," *New York Times,* February 3, 2014, *http://dealbook.nytimes.com/2014/02/03/too-many-sorry-excuses-for-apology/.*

customer confidence and trust have not been entirely restored. By 2015, Netflix had managed to regain some of the ground it had lost in measures of customer satisfaction, but its chief competitor, Amazon, had surged to the top.[9]

Should Hastings have done anything differently? The question can be answered by analyzing the text of the apology in light of the four ways of ethical thinking.

A general rule of thumb is that whenever a person uses just one or two ways of ethical thinking to justify a contentious decision, he or she will be criticized on the basis of the types of thinking not employed. What types of thinking did Hastings use? What types did he neglect? And what types of thinking did customers use in responding to him?

The Four-Way Method: Truth

Note that Hastings did not express regret for changing Netflix's business strategy, just for the way he communicated that strategy to customers. Hastings said, "I'm sorry," but he was sorry mainly for failing to communicate the reasons for the changes clearly and thoroughly. The underlying assumption is that customers' reactions to the changes were based on a false impression of the situation. Thus he drew primarily upon truth as he explained what Netflix was doing and why.

Hastings' message may have accurately diagnosed why customer response to the Netflix announcement was so negative, but to claim that he was issuing an apology was misleading. For one thing, it was not sincere. He was saying, in effect, "You have no legitimate reason to be angry with me." Even if that is correct, it makes the apology insincere. Everything said after that, all the reasons given to clear up the misunderstanding, was offered not as apology, but as excuse. That made the apology come off as patronizing to customers. Hastings seemed to assume that customers who are angry are also unreasonable, and that reassuring them with a calm voice and clear explanation would get them to see things properly and stop throwing a fit. But what if customers were reasonably angry? What if, for some customers at least, the changes by Netflix really were burdensome and

---

9. "The Foresee Experience Index: 2015 Retail Edition," *http://www.foresee.com /assets/ForeSee_FXI2015_Retail_Edition.pdf*.

unwelcome? That was the sentiment expressed by many customers, represented in this online comment by David Barba:

> This letter is disingenuous. You are offering an apology for not doing a good job of explaining the new structure but it is all about the needs for your corporation. What about the needs of the customer—that's what is missing here.[10]

That there was so little acknowledgment of legitimate customer concerns in the apology suggests that Hastings and his customers were still not "on the same page." Their respective perceptions of the situation were far apart. In fact, one gets the impression that the very conditions that prompted a hasty and ill-advised strategic move also prompted a hasty and ill-advised apology. It is unlikely that Hastings would have written the apology in the way he did if he had been listening carefully to his customers from the beginning.

The Four-Way Method: Consequences

What might customers have been legitimately angry about? Chiefly, they were angry about the negative consequences of the changes for them: namely, the considerable price increase and the inconvenience of having to subscribe to two separate services. Hastings addressed these consequences and more, highlighting the pros and the cons.

Netflix Consequences

Pros:

1. Separating the two services will allow Netflix to focus on the rapidly changing technology and market for streaming without being slowed down by maintaining compatibility with the DVD service.

Continued

---

10. Comment posted September 19, 2011, at 7:18 pm, *http://blog.netflix.com /2011/09/explanation-and-some-reflections.html.*

> **Netflix Consequences** Continued
>
> 2. Since each website will have a single focus, the sites will be easier for members to use.
> 3. Qwikster will be the same website and DVD service, just with different names.
> 4. Qwikster will add video games to its listings.
>
> Cons:
>
> 1. People who have an emotional attachment to the Netflix logo may feel some temporary loss with the name change on the DVD label ("I know that logo will grow on me over time, but still, it is hard").[11]
> 2. Ratings and reviews on one site will not show up on the other.
> 3. Members who wish to use both services will have to maintain subscription information on two sites instead of one.

Hastings did not address the reasons for the fee increase in his apology, but instead promised that there would be no more increases. "We're done with that," he stated simply. He had already discussed the fee increase at length in other places, and probably felt that customers, though not happy about it, nevertheless understood the need.

Addressing the consequences of a proposed controversial action in a straightforward fashion is very important, and Hastings deserves credit for devoting a substantial portion of his apology to the effects of the changes on Netflix and its customers. The problem is that they are not persuasive. In short, the "pros" do not outweigh the "cons." In fact, the "pros" do not even offer genuine benefits for the customer. Why can't Netflix respond to changing technology and markets for streaming right alongside the traditional DVD service? How will navigating two websites instead of one be easier for customers to use?

---

11. Ibid.

If the website and DVD service are really going to stay the same, why change the name? And why can't video games be added to the DVD service regardless of the split?

The "cons," on the other hand, do seem genuine. There are real inconveniences to customers in having to navigate two separate websites and maintain two separate subscriptions.

A typical response from customers was that of Christine Gunselman:

> This is stupid and will be a waste of my time. I was alright with the price increases because I understood that streaming is a huge cost. But splitting into two websites will lose all the convenience that is currently Netflix—instant and DVD rental. I will probably now cancel one of the services because I will not want to manage two sites. Terrible decision.[12]

Here is a case where the reasons given for the plan actually undermine the argument. Careful readers would have to conclude that either there are other reasons at work in the decision or Netflix should reverse its decision. When Netflix later scrapped the plan to spin off the DVD service and decided to continue providing both services under one name, it served as confirmation that the consequences detailed in the apology were not as significant as Hastings claimed.

The Four-Way Method: Fairness

It is interesting that many Netflix customers defended the changes by appealing to fairness, a strategy that Hastings himself did not employ. They pointed out that businesses have a right to increase prices, and customers have a right to either pay the fee or find a different provider. It is a contract to which neither side is forced.

Customer Jodi Bearden used that type of reasoning in her comment:

> I have kept up with the customer feedback over the past couple of months and while I have to say that I agree with

---

12. Ibid. Comment posted September 19, 2011, at 4:38 pm.

much of it, I cannot say that a company doesn't have the right to raise their prices as they deem necessary. Netflix is a business so let's talk business. It is not a responsibility or obligation to provide a service. As overhead and costs increase it sometimes becomes necessary to raise prices accordingly, that is how business works. Likewise, I have the right to discontinue my patronage at such a time that the cost of the service outweighs the benefit.[13]

But such a defense overlooks the fact that many Netflix customers do not regard themselves as simply purchasers of a service; they regard themselves as—in the company's own terminology—"members." And many long-term members, those who had been with the company from the beginning, who had helped build it by recommending it to their friends and acquaintances, felt they were being kicked out, downgraded to a second-rate club called "Qwikster," to something no longer worthy of the Netflix brand. Even the name suggested something ill-conceived and temporary, a fly-by-night operation, a scheme devised by a huckster.

Tim McClelland commented:

I have been a loyal customer since 2004. I thought that Net-flix was God's gift to home viewing, but little did I know that after years of loyalty you would continually stab me in the back. I was one of the few that stood by you when you raised your prices. I swore to my friends that it was okay. I understood that the economy was bad and we all need to make a profit, but shortly after raising your prices, you decide to do away with all aspects of convenience. You made me look like a fool when I stood by you on the price hike and now you have made yourselves the fool.

Splitting Netflix in two so that you have Netflix and Qwikster is the worst business decision since New Coke. I have never in my life written a complaint letter to a company, but you have forced my hand.[14]

---

13. Ibid. Comment posted September 20, 2011, at 9:51 am.
14. Ibid. Comment posted September 19, 2011, at 11:08 pm.

Customer loyalty is a form of trust, and trust is a two-edged sword. Trust is established over time by forging an ongoing relationship of mutuality. When one party is perceived as violating that mutuality, the repercussions are greater than if the trust had never existed. What Hastings did in his apology, by focusing on consequences and excluding any consideration of fairness, was to say, in effect, "It's just a business decision," to people who thought of themselves as more than just customers. Netflix tried to "have its cake and eat it too." That is, they tried to get the advantages of loyalty without being loyal to their membership. In short, customers felt as if Netflix had taken advantage of them by exploiting their commitment to the brand.

The Four-Way Method: Character

The one redeeming aspect of Hastings' apology is that he frankly acknowledged the character flaws that led to the negative customer reactions. He said that the company lacked "respect and humility" and that he, personally, "slid into arrogance." Thus he identified character flaws that needed to be changed in order to restore healthy relationships with customers. He did not speak passively and impersonally, claiming merely that "mistakes were made." Instead, he took responsibility, which is the first step in repairing a damaged relationship. That is most likely what customer Brian Wilkens alluded to when he commented, "It's big of you to offer an authentic apology."[15] But because Hastings apologized for the wrong things, he compounded the injury by exhibiting blindness to the very conditions that caused harm in the first place, as noted by Ed Jelinek: "No doubt your arrogance has opened up a perfect opportunity for me to support a new start-up elsewhere. Your letter of 'explanation' made your situation worse."[16]

Summary

An apology, to be successful, must be (a) a sincere expression of remorse and (b) signified by a genuine commitment not to repeat the offending or injurious behavior. Hastings' apology had the

---

15. Ibid. Comment posted September 20, 2011, at 12:17 pm.

16. Ibid. Comment posted September 19, 2011, at 8:04 pm.

markings of sincerity in that he accepted personal responsibility for the character traits that led to poor communication. Perhaps because sincere public apologies are so rare from leaders of large corporations, he received a great deal of praise from industry commentators. For example, Dov Seidman, the CEO of LRN, made these remarks during an interview:

> I think Reed Hastings really got it right, you know, when Netflix raised prices. Eight hundred thousand-or-so subscribers were irate, and they collectively bolted and left Netflix in forty-eight hours. And I think the first thing Reed did is, he went on an inward journey. . . . It was about . . . reclaiming . . . humility.[17]

But the apology failed to get a favorable response from many customers because it revealed an underlying insensitivity to their desires. It did not meet the second requirement of successful apologies: there was no commitment to changing the things about which customers were really upset. That requirement was not met until a short time later, when Netflix quietly announced that they would not split DVD and streaming services after all, thus proving true what Hastings had claimed: "actions speak louder than words."

Case Study 3: A Conflict of Interest?

Dawn Pendergast, a branch manager at Sunnycreek Community Bank,[18] has a decision to make. The bank recently revised its code of ethics, adopting a no-gift policy for all employees. Previously, the bank had a policy that prohibited employees from accepting gifts valued at more than $100, but it had been difficult to determine the value of some gifts, and there were a couple of employees at the bank who received many more gifts during the course of a year than others,

---

17. "The Fine Art of the Public Apology," *All Things Considered*, National Public Radio, February 4, 2014, *http://www.npr.org/2014/02/04/271591517/the-fine-art -of-the-public-apology*.

18. The characters and the bank in this case are fictional, but the events described in the case are real.

creating suspicion and some hard feelings among other employees. Dawn had been the one to suggest the new policy, arguing that banks depend on a reputation for fairness and integrity, and accepting gifts of any value could raise questions about the bank's motivations for approving or denying client loan applications. The president and the board agreed, and subsequently drafted the new guidelines. But now, just a week after approving the new policy, she has to decide what to do about a fruit basket.

Every year just before Christmas, the local Rotary Club sells fruit baskets as a fundraiser to support local charities. That morning, Jay, an insurance agent with an office across the street, a long-time customer of the bank and member of the Rotary Club, stopped by her office and placed a fruit basket on her desk. "Happy Holidays, Dawn!" Jerry announced brightly. "Sorry I can't stop to chat. I've got a whole carload of these to deliver." And with that he was out the door. As she watched him hurry out, it occurred to her: "I don't think I can accept this gift. What do I do now?"

The Four-Way Method: Truth

The first thing for Dawn to do is consider the broad context of the policy. Gift acceptance policies are designed to discourage conflicts of interest. A conflict occurs when a representative of an organization or profession has personal interests in the outcome of a decision that could sway his or her judgment away from purely professional considerations. If the personal interests actually do influence a decision, it is considered an "actual conflict of interest"; if personal interests are present, but they do not influence the decision, then it is considered a "potential conflict of interest." For example, when a purchaser for a company decides to sign a contract with Supplier A instead of Supplier B because Supplier A gives him season tickets to Chicago Cubs games, that would be an actual conflict of interest. But if the purchaser's judgment is not influenced by receiving the tickets (perhaps he is a White Sox fan), but still signs a contract with Supplier A (due to the superior quality of their products), then receiving tickets from Supplier A would merely be a potential conflict of interest.

Rules regarding conflicts of interest are central to most professional codes of ethics because there are so many ways in which personal interests can interfere with sound, responsible, professional judgment. And whenever that happens, the reputation of the entire profession can be harmed. If one basketball referee, for example, is caught accepting bribes to influence the outcome of a game, all referees are looked upon with suspicion. The public loses trust in the integrity of the game. When a banker is suspected of giving loans on favorable terms to personal friends and family members, investors may lose trust in the soundness of the bank's investments. Because of the effects on reputation, even potential conflicts of interest need to be taken seriously.

In the case under consideration, it is unlikely that the gift of a fruit basket would constitute an actual conflict of interest. After all, a few pieces of fruit are hardly sufficient incentive to unduly influence Dawn's professional judgment. And yet, Jerry is a client of the bank, and Dawn is in a position to make decisions regarding his accounts. Is it not possible that even a small gift could make her more favorably disposed toward Jerry, perhaps influencing her decisions in subtle ways? Just as important, is it not possible that someone might think her decisions were influenced by such a gift?

Jerry, however, is not thinking about these things when he delivers the fruit basket to Dawn. He is simply participating in an annual fundraiser for the good of the community. Every year, he gives a fruit basket to all neighboring businesses. It is his way of celebrating the holiday season, a small gesture of goodwill toward the people with whom he associates on a regular basis.

There are any number of things Dawn could do with the fruit basket, but three possibilities stand out. (1) She could accept the fruit basket, treating it as a harmless exception to the new no-gift policy. (2) She could give the fruit basket back to Jerry, thanking him for the kind gesture, but explaining that the bank's new policy does not allow her to keep it. (3) She could place the fruit basket in the break room with a note inviting all the bank's employees to enjoy it.

The Four-Way Method: Consequences

Although the gift is small, the actions Dawn takes in regard to it could affect a number of different people, including herself, Jerry, other bank employees, clients, and even the larger community.

Whenever new policies are put in place, employees in a company look to leadership to determine how they should be interpreted. It is one thing to know what a policy *says*, it is another thing altogether to know what it *means* in a particular context. For that reason, Dawn's response to this gift is significant, because it is the first opportunity for employees to witness how she interprets the no-gift policy. If she accepts the gift with no explanation, or even if she says something like, "Oh, the policy was never intended for this type of thing," it could create confusion. What does "this type of thing" mean, any-way? Gifts worth less than $20? Seasonal gifts? Food items? Gifts given to the branch manager? Dawn may know what she means by "this sort of thing," but how is everyone else supposed to know? The results of such confusion will not really be tested until Dawn is put in the position of enforcing the policy when applied to one of her employees. The response is sure to come back to her: "But what do you mean I can't accept this certificate to Maxie's? I thought the pol-icy didn't apply to food?"

Returning the gift is also problematic, however. For one thing, there are Jerry's feelings to consider. After all, she does not want to convey the message that the bank is ungrateful for his business or even that she does not appreciate his kindness. She can explain the situation to Jerry, but still, returning a gift is awkward. The bigger problem is that the Rotary Club depends on the annual fruit basket sale as their chief fundraising event, and the proceeds support worthy causes in the community. Does she want word to get around that her bank will no longer participate in fundraisers like this one? Will her rejection of the gift be taken as implied criticism of other businesses that happily accept fruit baskets every year? Dawn knows how gossip spreads in small communities, and she has been around long enough to know that if she returns the fruit basket to Jerry, Rotarians will talk about it. She does not want a policy intended to protect the bank's reputation to end up dam-aging it instead.

So considering all the potential consequences, it seems best to find a way of accepting the gift without keeping it for herself. It looks like putting the basket in the break room to share with all employees is an option that would be beneficial to all concerned.

The Four-Way Method: Fairness

The first thing that occurs to Dawn when she thinks about fairness is that she must make sure she is following the bank's rules and guidelines in precisely the same fashion that she expects of other employees. She cannot make an exception in this case just because she is the branch manager. So she performs a series of thought experiments. What would she think if Joe (a mortgage lender at the bank) received a fruit basket and did not report it? Well, she would certainly ask him why he didn't. She might even begin to question whether there were other bank policies that Joe was inclined to interpret broadly and about which he was keeping silent. What would she think if Joe received a fruit basket and then returned it to the giver? It wouldn't lead her to question Joe's integrity, but it might cause her to question his judgment and his skill in dealing with clients. She realized that in neither case—Joe keeping it for himself or returning it—would she form an impression she would want others to form of her.

Another thought occurs to her. If she wants to treat her employees the way she would want to be treated, why not use this situation as a learning opportunity? She could let them participate in the decision about what to do with the fruit basket. Perhaps they would come up with an idea that had not yet occurred to her, and it would demonstrate that she respects and values their participation and input, even about a decision she could easily make by herself.

The Four-Way Method: Character

The old adage "actions speak louder than words" is especially pertinent when it comes to assessing character. If Dawn returns the gift to Jerry, she will appear ungrateful, regardless of what she tries to say. Perhaps she would appear personally ungrateful. What's worse, however, is that she is acting as a representative of the bank, and her actions speak to the character of the bank. The bank has a plaque hanging prominently in the lobby, listing its core values. Ingratitude is not among them. However, "service to the community" is listed on that plaque, along with "integrity." What can Dawn do in this instance that will demonstrate those values?

To act with integrity, she must not only abide by the new policy, she must be seen to embrace it in both letter and spirit. Accepting the gift for herself is not an option, nor is returning the gift, especially if she wants to demonstrate service to the community. When Dawn thinks about it in this way, she realizes that she has to accept the gift graciously and yet do it in a way that does not violate the policy. And the only way to do this is to accept it on behalf of others.

Dawn understands that she needs to set an example for her employees. She may not be the bank president, but the people she works with look up to her. Whether she acknowledges it consciously or not, she serves as a role model, especially for some of the younger tellers who have confided in her about their future hopes and sought her advice on advancing their careers. Even seemingly trivial decisions, like what to do about a fruit basket, may loom large in their minds as they form crucial early impressions about how to be a professional in the banking industry.

Summary

Ethics policies in companies are generally adopted in response to problems that have occurred in the past or in anticipation of problems that might arise in the future. But they frequently fail to fit present situations in precisely the ways that are intended. So policies have to be revisited occasionally: modified, expanded, contracted, or repealed.

In some ways, the case of the fruit basket is not a "big deal." Dawn is able to think through the issue and quickly come to a solution that is reasonable and acceptable. But it points to the possibility that the no-gift policy, which seemed so straightforward and simple to implement when she first proposed it, may in fact be too broad. What other situations might arise that she had not considered? Would they all be as easy to work through as the fruit basket was? Dawn decides that she is going to take a closer look at gift policies adopted by other banks. What kinds of exceptions do they provide for in their policies? What can she learn from the experience of other institutions?

Conclusion

It is natural to want to find the "right" answer to every ethical conflict, and it is sometimes possible to do so. But it is not possible in every case because there are different ways of evaluating what is "right" or "good." Sometimes, in really challenging cases, the best that can be done is to consider all the possible options and come up with a solution that fits the criteria (truth, consequences, fairness, and character) better than other available options.

What makes ethical decision making especially difficult is that the people who are responsible for the decisions are usually emotionally involved in some way: the outcome of the decision may have a significant impact on one's friends, financial well-being, or reputation. When one is involved in a situation, even indirectly, it is hard to maintain an unbiased perspective.

That is why the most important part of ethical decision making is the ability to have constructive, honest conversations with others. That allows one to take advantage of what is sometimes called "common sense," the sense that results from a number of people working in common to resolve a problem. Other people may be able to formulate solutions that one does not envision; others might place emphasis on a way of ethical thinking that one has overlooked.

Common sense in the workplace is the key feature of any ethical business culture. Competent, sensible, constructive ethical deliberation cannot take place without it. But common sense does not result by happenstance. It is the natural product of the deep trust that develops over time when people are all in alignment and working in harmony.

Discussion Questions

1. Identify situations in your workplace or in your university to which you could apply the Four-Way Method.

2. Of the four ways of ethical thinking, which one do you rely on most to make difficult decisions?

3. Think about stories you have heard or read about recently in which a business was involved in an ethical scandal. Apply the Four-Way Method to find a way in which that scandal might have been avoided.

Resources for Further Exploration

PRINT

Gentile, Mary C. *Giving Voice to Values: How to Speak Your Mind When You Know What's Right.* New Haven, CT: Yale University Press, 2010.

> One of the chief tasks of a business ethics course is helping students move beyond the analysis of hypothetical ethical situations to preparing for those occasions when they have to act. Gentile, of Babson College, describes an innovative approach to addressing the implementation of ethical practices in this book.

OTHER MEDIA

"Ethics Cases." Markkula Center for Applied Ethics at Santa Clara University. *http://www.scu.edu/ethics/practicing/focusareas/cases.cfm ?fam=BUSI.*

> This is another good website for business ethics cases.

"Ethics Unwrapped." McCombs School of Business at the University of Texas. *http://ethicsunwrapped.utexas.edu/videos.*

> The McCombs School of Business has produced a series of forty-eight short, engaging videos illustrating key concepts in business ethics.

Gentile, Mary C. *The Giving Voice to Values Curriculum. http://www. babson.edu/Academics/teaching-research/gvv/Pages/home.aspx.*

> This website, by the author of *Giving Voice to Values*, contains a wealth of resources for students and instructors alike, including readings, teaching modules, and a number of cases that can be used in the classroom.

The Insider. Directed by Michael Mann. Burbank, CA: Touchstone Home Entertainment, 2000. Time: 02:37:00.

> Movies that can be used to generate discussion of ethical issues are too numerous to list. The one cited here, however, is particularly useful. This movie tells the story of Jeffrey Wigand, a research biologist for the tobacco company Brown and Williamson, and his decision to do a whistle-blowing interview for

60 Minutes producer Lowell Bergman. Several characters in the film, especially Wigand and Bergman, face a series of high-stakes ethical choices, allowing the viewer to witness how the different ways of ethical thinking come into play.

Red Gold. Directed by Travis Rummel and Ben Knight. Denver: Felt Sole Media, 2009. Time: 00:55:00.

This documentary depicts the controversy in Bristol Bay, Alaska, over the proposed Pebble Mine. Interviews with mining advocates, commercial fishermen, and Native Alaskans illustrates how truth, consequences, fairness, and character are used by all sides to express their positions on the issue. The cinematography is outstanding.

Conclusion

Recall the question that opened this book: What does it mean for an organization to be ethical? Although there is still much to say on the subject, the answer, developed over the last five chapters, can be summarized this way:

Every organization has three parts: mind, body, and spirit. For a person or organization to be good, these parts must each perform their function well and work together in harmony. The virtues corresponding to each part are wisdom, temperance, and courage, and when these virtues coexist, the result is integrity. An ethical organization is an organization with integrity.

To put this in more conventional terms, one can speak of mind as *why* the organization does what it does (its mission or purpose), body as *what* or *who* comprises the organization (its resources, especially people), and spirit as *how* the organization conducts itself (its rules, policies, and procedures).

An ethical organization then, one in which each part is performing its function well, must first of all have a *good purpose*, that is, it must be formed in order to do something worthwhile, something in which people find meaning and to which they can feel justified in dedicating a substantial portion of their lives. Second, it must be comprised of *good people*, that is, people of sound character who believe in the shared purpose of the organization and have sufficient virtue to contribute to it through their daily behavior. Finally, it must have a *good organizational structure*, that is, it must have rules, policies, and procedures that support the organization's purpose, implemented in a way that employees recognize as fair; otherwise, they may become dispirited and disengaged.

Ethical decision making is not something extra, added on top of all these things. Rather, it is just what happens when good people work together to make responsible decisions within an ethical business.

More often than not, however, organizations fail in some respect with regard to purpose, people, and structure. Conflict arises, people get frustrated with the leadership or with their coworkers, strategies that once looked promising begin to unravel, well-intentioned policies turn out to have unexpected and regrettable outcomes for some. It is when such failures occur that ethical decision making is most crucial, and some agreed-upon method for conducting difficult discussions is necessary to maintain focus and goodwill.

The Four-Way Method is designed to help people at every level of an organization engage in constructive discussions about serious issues. Using language that is already familiar, this approach acknowledges that people engage in moral reasoning every day; what they need is some agreed-upon method to help them avoid the pitfalls of moral disengagement and partial engagement that can either create or exacerbate misunderstandings.

There are five broad types of application for the Four-Way Method in organizations:

1. Resolving Conflicts: Conflicts can arise at every level of an organization, so knowing how to participate in constructive discussions that maintain goodwill among all participants, from CEOs to custodians, is something everyone needs.

2. Planning: Healthy organizations anticipate potential problems in advance, and the Four-Way Method can be used by leadership teams to think thoroughly about the ethical implications of a proposed action before it is implemented.

3. Training: Regular practice in using all four ways of ethical thinking to work through hypothetical situations or to review past problematic situations is especially helpful for those whose work tends to generate significant differences of opinion.

4. Communicating: Whenever a project or proposal is announced that has significant effects on others, it is helpful to consider carefully in advance how the announcement will be perceived by the intended audience. The Four-Way Method can be useful in crafting language that addresses all four ways of ethical thinking.

5. Reflecting: The first step in ethical maturity is acknowledging one's own tendencies for bias and partiality, particularly when it comes to generating reasons justifying one's actions. The Four-Way Method may be used as a corrective to partiality, helping one to carefully consider ways of thinking about a problem that one would otherwise overlook.

Creating and sustaining an ethical organization requires hard work and persistence, not just by leadership, but by everyone involved. And constant attention must be paid especially to the ways in which people talk to, with, and about one another. After all, we create our communities by the conversations we have. Every potential crisis is an opportunity to strengthen and rebuild relationships and restore trust by affirming a commitment to listen to one another and by attending to the ways people think about truth, consequences, fairness, and character.

Index

Note: An 'n', 's', or 't' following a page number indicates a footnote, sidebar, or table, respectively

A

abuse, 72
accidents. *see* safety
Adams, Scott, 89
administrative assistant example, 91
advantageous comparison, 113
advice, 30–31, 103, 138, 139, 141, 142, 143
"alternate dispute resolution," 13–14
altruism, 28, 53, 88
anti-Semitism, 114
apologies, 144–152. *see also* Netflix case study
Arendt, Hannah, 91, 119n12
Ariely, Dan, 27, 28
Aristotle, 8, 53n16, 72, 99–100, 119n12, 126
Arndt, Jerry, 102–103
arts and crafts, 95n38
assumptions, 28, 29, 47, 67, 109, 122, 142, 146
AT&T, 52, 80
Augustine of Hippo, 23–25, 32
Auschwitz, 59–60
authority, 101–102, 138–139. *see also* leadership; power

B

Bandura, Albert, 112–113
bank case study, 152–157
bankruptcy example, 56s–58s
Barba, David, 147
Bartleby the Scrivener, 89
basketball foul example, 110–111

Baum, L. Frank, 19
Bearden, Jodi, 149–150
Behar, Howard, 82
Bentham, Jeremy, 123
blame, 10, 113, 114
bodies, 18–19, 63, 161
Bois, Jon, 85–86
bonuses, 25–26, 29–30, 63, 85
boomerang theory, 127s
brake components example, 56s–58s
bribes, 11, 154
Broetje, Cheryl and Ralph, 60s–62s
Broetje Orchards, 61s–62s
Bugbee, Henry, 102n44
bullying, 78, 82, 91
burnout, 94, 99–100

C

Calley, William, 113n6
cardinal virtues, 17–19
"carrot and stick" approach, 30
Carter, Nancy, 88n26
case studies, 134, 135. *see also* moral imagination; *specific case studies*
Categorical Imperative, 125
causes *versus* reasons, 46–47
Center for Applied Ethics, 53
CEO pay packages, 87
change, 65–66
Chaplin, Charlie, 43
Chappell, Tom, 34
character. *see also* virtues
    bank case study and, 156–157
    communities of, 30–39

compliance and, 22–23
ethical organizations and, 161
ethical reasoning and, 109,
122n17
financial incentives and, 27–28
Four-Way Method and,
125–126, 129–130
good workplaces and, 31–32
listening and, 56
Netflix case study and, 151
policies and, 27
power and, 78–80
trust and, 87
whistle-blower case study and,
142
chores, 95
circles of life, 96s–97s
civic engagement, 97s–99s
classroom *versus* reality, 9–10
climate change example, 122
Clinical Ethics (Jonsen, Siegler, and
Winslade), 119n14
Club Aluminum Company,
117s–119s
codes, 21–22
coercive power, 54–55, 75, 78–79,
85–86, 130. *see also* power
college student/advisor example, 93
Collins, Jeff, 32
commitment, 33, 35, 52. *see also*
common good
common good, 52–53, 58, 60, 63,
88, 132. *see also* commitment
common sense, 158
communication, 50, 129–130,
145, 162–163. *see also* listening;
perception; persuasion
compliance, 11, 21–30, 39
computers, 41–42. *see also*
technology
Confessions (Augustine), 23–24
confidence, 83–84, 90
conflicts. *see also* self-interest

ethical organizations and,
161–162
ethics and, 8
Four-Way Method and, 129, 162
of interest, 152–158
policies and, 72n2
purpose and, 60
consent, 78
consequences
bank case study and, 154–155
distortion of, 113
Four-Way Method and, 76–77,
122–123, 129
Netflix case study and, 147–149
sleepover example and, 114–115,
116
whistle-blower case study and,
139–141
consequentialism, 119n12
construction site example, 71
contexts, 26–27, 72, 121–122,
138–139, 153. *see also* ethical
culture
courage, 17–18, 22, 28, 39, 91, 142,
161
cowardice, 26
creative activities, 95
crises, 106–108
custodian examples, 22–23, 30
customer loyalty, 144, 150, 151
cynicism, 9–10

D

debt, 93
deception, 78. *see also* self-deception
decision making. *see also* Four-Way
Method; reasoning, ethical
common sense and, 158
ethical culture and, 10, 12
ethical organizations and,
161–162
Four-Way method and, 131–132

joint, 130–132
light fixture example and, 105–108
mind and, 18
power and, 83
Taylor/Club Aluminum and, 117s–119s
deep stories, 33–35, 36s–37s
dehumanization, 114
Delphi Automotive brake assembly, 56s–58s
Delta Airlines, 15–16
deontology, 119n12
De Pree, Max, 38
desires, 18, 25–26, 27, 28. *see also* inclinations; self-interest
Desk Set (movie), 41–42
dignity, 43, 103. *see also* respect
Dilbert, 89
disagreement, 131. *see also* conflicts; self-interest
disconnected organization, 66–67
discrimination, 72, 73s–74s, 78, 101
disengagement. *see* moral disengagement
dishonesty, 126
drill press collapse case study, 135–144
Driscoll, Chuck, 72s–74s
Drucker, Peter F., 30, 30n24
Duet, William U., 65
Duncan, David James, 102

E

egos, 90n31
Eichmann, Adolf, 119n12
elephant and rider analogy, 112
emotions, 18
ends, 76–77
ends in themselves, 48, 69, 79
energy, 95, 96s–97s

engagement. *see also* moral disengagement
friends and, 100
listening and, 56
partial, 114, 119–120, 131, 162
trust and, 88–92
Enron, 15–16, 28–29, 84
equality, 123–124
Ericsson, K. Anders, 108
"ethical," 7
ethical culture, 39, 67–68, 161–162. *see also* character; compliance; contexts; decision making; Four-Way Method; leadership; meaning; virtues
ethical theories, 8, 119–120, 138. *see also* utilitarianism; virtue ethics
eudaimonia, 126n21
euphemistic language, 113
exceptions, 72
exercise, 95
exit, 88–89
expectations, 21
expert power, 76, 108

F

fairness
bank case study and, 156
ethical organizations and, 161
Four-Way Method and, 123–125, 129
Netflix case study and, 149–151
power and, 77–78
respect and, 124
sleepover example and, 115, 116
whistle-blower case study and, 141–142
Fast, Nathanael, 82
fathers and sons, 101–102, 114–116
favoritism, 101
fear, 28, 29, 55, 57s, 88, 90
financial incentives, 27–28

flourishing, 7, 8, 16, 38, 53n16, 102, 126n21. *see also* ethical culture
focus, lack of, 66–67
force. *see* power
Ford, Henry, 42
forgiveness, 91–92
Four-Way Method. *see also* character; consequences; fairness; truth
    application of, 128–132, 162–163
    bank case study and, 152–157
    basketball foul example and, 110–111
    effectiveness of, 119
    ethical thinking and, 119–120
    illustrated, 121s
    light fixture falling example and, 131–132
    Taylor example and, 118s–119s
    whistle-blower case study and, 135–144
Frankl, Victor, 59–60
fraud, 28–29, 84, 113n7
French, John R.P., 75–76
Frey, Bruno, 27
friendship, 24, 25, 45, 99–102, 106–107
"From Surviving to Thriving" (Duet), 65

G

Gallup polls, 83, 83–84t, 89
Gandhi, 76
Garver, Newton, 55
General Electric engineer, 96s–98s
General Motors. *see* Delphi Automotive brake assembly
George, Bill, 87
German workers, 99
gift policies, 72n2, 125, 152–157
Gladwell, Malcolm, 108n2

Gneezy, Uri, 27
Golden Rule, 123–124, 142
good and bad, 109, 119, 158
good life, 7–8
good organizations, 16
goodwill, 14, 130, 162
good work, 7–8, 10
good workplaces, 31–32, 33
greed, 26, 28, 29, 113
Greek workers, 99
Green, Tom, 56s–58s
Greenleaf, Robert, 67
Greenleaf, Robert K., 51–54, 56, 58–59, 80–81, 82, 90
grocery business example, 126s–128s
Grounding for the Metaphysics of Morals (Kant), 48
growth, human, 59, 67
Gunselman, Christine, 149

H

Haidt, Jonathan, 112
happiness, 8, 33, 53n16, 126
harassment, 63–64, 72, 78, 101
hardhat example, 71
Hastings, Reed, 144
Haughey, John, 33n28, 37
Hawthorne Studies, 42–45, 51, 52
Hayman, James, 27
headlines example, 111
health care settings, 119n14. *see also* hospital janitor case; hospital nurse case; nursing home fraud example
Heifetz, Ronald, 135
Helming, Oscar C., 51, 53
Hemstead, Louise, 19s–21s
Herman Miller company, 38
Herzberg, Frederick, 92–93
Hesse, Herman, 59
Heyman, James, 28

hierarchies, 81
Hirschman, Albert O., 88
honesty, 126, 130. *see also* sincerity;
   truth
hope, 55–56, 144
hospital janitor case, 22
hospital nurse case, 99
how, 63, 161
Hubbard, Elbert, 95n38
human growth, 67
human nature. *see also* subjective/
   objective nature
   coercive power and, 78–80
   hope and, 56
   leadership and, 45–51, 54–55
   policies and, 72
   purpose and, 60
   servant leadership and, 54
   virtues and, 18
humility, 90, 145, 151, 152

I

identity, 32, 35, 37–38
ignorance, 25–27, 28, 29
Iliad, The; or, The Poem of Force
   (Weil), 78
inclinations, 111–112. *see also*
   desires; self-interest
injustice, 26–27
institutions, 51–52, 53–54
integrity. *see also* Hemstead, Louise
   advice and, 31
   bank case study and, 156, 157
   bribes and, 154
   civic life and, 99s
   as core value, 15–17
   ethical organizations and, 161
   financial systems and, 26
   leaders and, 87
   Netflix and, 144
   trust and, 88
   wisdom and, 28, 39

intentional/unintentional behavior,
   47
intuitions, ethical, 112, 116
Inventing America (Wills), 54–55
Israeli judges example, 49

J

J.C. Penney, 87
Jefferson, Thomas, 54–55, 56
Jeffreys, Greg, 114n8
Jelinek, Ed, 151
Johnson, Ronald, 87
Jonsen, Albert R., 119n14
Journey to the East, The (Hesse), 59
justice, 17–18, 100–101
justification, moral, 113, 116

K

Kant, Immanuel, 48, 78n6, 79,
   119nn12,13, 125
Kasser, Tim, 28n20

L

language, 95, 113, 162
L'Arche, 33
laws, 78
lawsuits, 13–14, 38
Lay, Ken, 28–29
layoff examples, 41, 65, 88
leadership. *see also* Hawthorne
   Studies; listening; power;
   purpose; virtues
   bank case study and, 155, 157
   commitment to common good
      and, 52
   compliance frameworks and, 30
   De Pree on, 38
   dignity and respect and, 41–42,
      68–69
   Driscoll example, 72s–74s

false assumptions and, 29–30
human nature and, 45–51, 54–55
mission and, 63
productivity and, 50
purpose and, 59–68
relationships and, 31, 101–103
servant leadership, 51–59,
    56s–58s, 127s–128s
subjective/objective natures and,
    68–69
virtue and, 53, 56
legitimate power, 76
leisure, 96–97
Letters to the Editor example,
    111–112
licorice sharing example, 124–125
light bulb example, 46–47
light fixture falling example,
    105–108, 131–132
listening
    brake assembly plant example,
        57s
    eliciting voice and, 90–92
    engagement and, 56
    ethical reasoning and, 116
    Four-Way Method and, 163
    grocery store leader example
        and, 128s
    mission focus and, 68
    power and, 80–81, 91, 103
low blood sugar example, 49
loyalty of customers, 144, 150, 151
loyalty to company, 86

M

machines, 43, 51. *see also* computers;
    Hawthorne Studies; technology
Madoff, Bernard, 113n7
manipulation, 78, 85
Man's Search for Meaning (Frankl),
    59–60
markets, monetary and social, 28

Marshalls, 72s–74s
Marvin, Jake, 88
Marvin, Susan, 35s–37s
Marvin Windows and Doors,
    35s–37s, 88
Mayo, Elton, 45
McClelland, Tim, 150
McGregor, Douglas, 29–30
McNeely, Eugene, 80
meaning. *see also* purpose
    burnout and, 94, 95
    circle of life and, 9, 96s–97s
    ethical organizations and, 161
    friendship and, 99–102
    Hawthorne Studies and, 51
    motivation and, 30, 92–102
    purpose and, 63
    servant leaders and, 59
    stories and, 37
mediation, 14
Medicare fraud example, 8–10
Medtronic, 87
Melrose, Ken, 13, 14
Melville, Herman, 89
methyl chloride effects, 140–141
Microsoft, 15–16
Miller, Mary, 56s–58s
minds, 18–19, 46, 60, 63, 161. *see
    also* rationality
mission disengagement example,
    66–67
mission-focused organizations, 63,
    64, 67–68, 161
Modern Times (movie), 43–44
Monopoly (game) example, 124
moral disengagement
    burnout and, 94
    character and, 27
    Dilbert cartoon and, 89
    fairness and, 161
    Four-Way Method and, 120, 162
    ignorance, greed, and fear and,
        29

mechanisms of, 113–116
power case study and, 66
reasoning and, 131
voice and, 90
moral imagination
described, 134–135
gift to bank manager case study, 152–158
Netflix case study and, 144–152
whistle-blower case study and, 135–144
motivation. *see also* financial incentives; self-interest
Augustine's example and, 23–24
character and, 125
coercive power and, 85–86
intrinsic/extrinsic, 28n20
leadership and, 55
meaning and, 30, 92–102
social, 28
whistle-blower case study and, 142
wise leader and, 30
My Lai Massacre, 113n6

N

Netflix case study, 144–152
Nicomachean Ethics (Aristotle), 99–100, 126. *see also* Aristotle
Nietzsche, 59–60
nurse case, 99
nursing home fraud example, 8–10

O

Oberholzer-Gee, Felix, 27
objective/subjective nature, 46, 47, 68, 78
O'Neill, Onora, 119n12
optimism, 55–56
options, 123, 158. *see also* moral imagination

orchard example, 61s–62s
organic food, 20s
Organic Valley, 19s–21s
organizational structure, 161

P

partial engagement, 114, 119–120, 162
partiality, 101, 162–163
pay ratios, 87
pear-stealing example, 23–24
pencil-in-mouth example, 48
Pennock, George, 44
"people," 32
perception, 56, 122, 147. *see also* communication
perspectives, 123–124, 134–135, 158
persuasion
decision making and, 108
Four-Way Method and, 119
leadership and, 53, 80–81
Netflix case study and, 148–149
Pettigrew, Mark, 105–107
phronēsis, 72
planning, 162
Platinum Rule, 124n19
Plato, 17–18. *see also* Socrates
policies. *see also* compliance; gift policies
bank case study and, 153, 155, 157
character and, 27
decision making and, 117s–118s
ethical organizations and, 11, 161
friendship and, 101
human nature and, 72
leadership and, 102
limits of, 21–22
Netflix and, 144
Polk, Sam, 25–26
power. *see also* leadership; trust

character and, 78–80
coercive, 54–55, 75, 78–79, 85–86, 130
decision making and, 83
defined, 63, 75–76
expert, 76, 108
fairness and, 77–78
limits of, 82–84
listening and, 80–81, 91, 103
persuasion and, 80–82
power-led organizations, 65–66
relationships and, 101–103
servant leadership and, 54–55
trust and, 31, 103
practice, 108
preventive orientation, 10
Price, Donna, 73s–74s
principle of subsidiarity, 81n14
productivity, 100. *see also* Hawthorne Studies
profit, 32, 36s, 43, 67, 68–69
promising, 91
punishment, 29–30
purpose, 32–33, 59–68, 63, 91, 100, 161. *see also* meaning; stories

R

Radio Shack, 85–86
Randolph, Marc, 144
Rath, Tom, 100
rationality, 45–46, 48–50, 60. *see also* ethical theories; Four-Way Method; minds
Raven, Bertram, 75–76
reactive orientation, 10
real estate scam, 114n8
real world, 9–10
reasoning, ethical. *see also* decision making; Four-Way Method
Augustine on, 23–24
choosing sides and, 111–112
ease of, 108–111

moral disengagement and, 113–116
reasons *versus* causes, 46–47
referent power, 76
reflection, 68, 79–80, 115, 116, 131, 134–135, 162. *see also* moral imagination
regulations, 26
relationships. *see also* friendship; power; subjective/objective nature; trust
Augustine on, 24
character and, 126
decision making and, 132
Desk Set and, 41–42
energy and, 95
ethical culture and, 14–16
forgiveness and, 91
Four-Way Method and, 163
grocery store example and, 127s
leaders and, 31
orchard example and, 62s
power and, 101–103
whistle-blower case study and, 142
remorse, 13
Republic (Plato), 17–18
research, empirical, 82
resource-led organizations, 63–64
respect. *see also* dignity
bank case study and, 156
consent and, 78
fairness and, 124
Hawthorne Studies and, 51
Netflix case study and, 145, 151
reverence and, 101
sleepover example and, 115
whistle-blower case study and, 142
responsibility
displacement/diffusion of, 113
displacement of, 113
intentions and, 47

listening and, 91
motivation and, 93
Netflix case study and, 151
restructuring examples, 65–66, 129.
  see also structures, organizational
reverence, 101
rewards, 29–30, 75–76
right and wrong, 109, 119, 158
*Righteous Mind: Why Good People
  Are Divided by Politics and
  Religion, The* (Haidt), 111–112
River Runs Through It, A (movie),
  101–102
rules, 21–22, 23, 27, 71–72
Rustichini, Aldo, 27

S

safety, 71, 105–107, 135–144. *see
  also* light fixture falling example;
  whistle-blower case study
Saline, Lindon "Lindy," 97s–99s
school, 97, 98s, 98s–99s
seasonal workers, 61s–62n
Seidman, Dov, 152
self-deception, 25, 27, 122
self-interest. *see also* conflicts;
    Golden Rule
  bank case study and, 153–154
  communication and, 130
  consequences and, 123
  four way method and, 129
  licorice sharing example and,
    124–125
  power and, 68
self-reflection, 129
self-respect, 48
Servant as Leader, The (Greenleaf),
  52–53, 59n25
servant leadership, 51–59, 56s–58s,
  127s–128s
shame, 85
Siegler, Mark, 119n14

sincerity, 11, 53, 91, 103, 116,
  151–152. *see also* apologies;
  honesty
Skogen, Dave, 126s–128s
slavery, 79
sleep, 99
sleepover example, 114–115,
  115–116
Smartest Guys in the Room, The
  (McLean and Elking), 29
Social Bases of Power, The (French
  and Raven), 75–76
social networking, 97s
Sociometric Solutions, 50
Socrates, 122. *see also* Plato
Soul of a Business, The (Chappell), 34
spirit, 18–19, 63, 65–66, 161
Starbucks North America, 82
Stoll, Clarence, 44
stories, 12, 33–35, 36s–37s, 37–38,
  45
strategic planning example, 66–67
structures, organizational, 75,
  81, 161. *see also* restructuring
  examples
subjective/objective nature, 46, 47,
  68–69, 78
subsidiarity, principle of, 81n14
Sunnycreek Community Bank case
  study, 152–157

T

Taylor, Frederick Winslow, 42–44,
  51, 68–69
Taylor, Herbert J., 117s–119s
technology, 49–50. *see also* computers; machines
television, 95
telos, 60, 60n28
temperance, 17–18, 28, 39, 161
"ten-thousand-hour rule," 108n2
Thao, Julie, 99

"Theories X and Y," 29–30
Thompson, Darrell, 118s–119s
Thoreau, H. D., 8
threats, 29–30
Three Little Pigs, The, 16–17
thriving, 90
Tom's of Maine, 34–35
Toro Company example, 13, 30, 38
training
    bankruptcy example and,
      57s–58s
    compliance and, 21
    decision making and, 107
    Driscoll example, 73s
    Four-Way Method and, 162
    trust and, 86
    values and, 23–24
    whistle-blower case study and,
      139
Trane (manufacturing company),
    102–103
treadmills, 50
trust
    American attitudes and, 83–85,
      91–92
    bank case study and, 154
    bankruptcy example and, 58s
    common sense and, 158
    community of character and, 31
    decision-making and, 106–107
    engagement and, 88–92
    Four-Way Method and, 130
    honesty and, 126
    lie detection and, 88n26
    Medicare fraud example and,
      9–10
    motivation and, 85–86
    Netflix case study and, 146, 151
    power and, 31, 103
    Toro Company and, 13–14
    virtues and, 86–88
    whistle-blower case study and,
      142

truth. *see also* contexts
    bank case study and, 153–154
    Four-Way Method and, 76,
      121–122, 129
    Netflix case study and,
      146–147
    whistle-blower case study and,
      137–138

U

unethical business culture, 11, 29
utilitarianism, 123

V

values, 23–24. *see also* meaning;
    purpose; virtues
Vanier, Jean, 33
Verizon, 16
vices, 15–16, 126
victims, blame of, 114
video games, 97s
virtue ethics, 8n2
virtues. *see also* character; friendship;
    wisdom *and other virtues*
    cardinal, 17–19
    character and, 126
    classical, 13–21
    compliance and, 22
    ethical culture and, 69
    leadership and, 53, 56
    stories and, 12
    trust and, 86–88
Vital Friends (Rath), 100
voice, 79, 81–82, 88–90
volunteering, 97s. *see also* civic
    engagement

W

Waber, Ben, 50
Wall Street trader, 25–26

wealth, 25–26
Weber, J. Mark, 88n26
weekends, 95
Weil, Simone, 78–80, 82
what, 63, 161
whistle-blower case study, 135–144
whistle-blowers, 11–12. *see also*
    courage
"*Who Moved My Cheese*" (Johnson),
    65
why, 63, 161
Wilkens, Brian, 151
Wills, Garry, 54–55
Winslade, William J., 119n14
wisdom. *see also* integrity; persuasion
    Enron and, 29
    ethical organizations and, 161

    janitor examples and, 22–23
    motivation and, 30
    Plato and, 17–18
    rules and, 72
    Three Little Pigs and, 16–17
    trust and, 88
    whistle-blower case study and,
        142
wisdom, practical, 72
Wizard of Oz, The (Baum), 19
work hours, average U.S., 7
work-life balance, 93, 94–99
WorldCom, 84

Y

YMCA logo, 18*i*–19